Other Books by N.S. Diaz

The Song That Was Never Written
(A book of poetic thoughts)

Their Song
(Poetic Thoughts)

Beyond the Mist
(Short Stories)

Bathing Suits, Bubble Bath and Battleships

N.S. Diaz

PublishAmerica
Baltimore

First printing

PublishAmerica has allowed this work to remain exactly as the author intended, verbatim, without editorial input.

ISBN: 1-60563-254-6
PUBLISHED BY PUBLISHAMERICA, LLLP
www.publishamerica.com
Baltimore

Printed in the United States of America

Dedication

To my husband—for your childhood memories,
too!
To my sons—who have learned a lot
from my childhood stories.
For my sister, and my brothers.
In memory of my loving parents and my Aunt
Margie.

My prayers to the innocent victims
and their families for the
September 11th tragedy in 2001...

Note from Author

Shortly after writing this book, my Norwegian elkhound passed away. I just need to say that I miss my lovely Sheba...each and every day.

Some years later, a homeless kitten followed me into my home and she has never left my side. Her name is Mimi. She is as beautiful as a new dawn...

Being "street wise" is most likely something that cannot be taught. It can't be found in a classroom. Sometimes, it can't even be taught at home.

One has to have actually have "lived" it! Just like if one is self educated or college educated. They can read many books. But the true experience to any field or life achievement has to be actual "hands on."

I have a childhood memory of someone I knew a very long time ago. She grew up in a place where one truly had to learn how to survive. She is almost fifty years old now. She raised two children in suburbia. Throughout their lives, she has shared with them her life experiences. She does believe that her stories to them have made them less naive, less vulnerable. She simply taught them, among other things, survival. And of this, she knows first hand!

Manhattan! The Lower East Side of New York City—the Chinatown area. Some call it "The Wall Street" area.

But the most fascinating of all was the place

where I grew up, remembering my early childhood years in The Smith Projects!

My story begins through the eyes of a three year old little girl as she "sees" the world. Her face to face knowledge of what it truly is for a tiny child to grow up through many challenges.

This is her life of what is "real." Not T.V. sitcoms. This is a tale of a little girl's memories, the way that she remembers...

I was born in a Manhattan Hospital. Six whole pounds! I was not quite eighteen inches in length. That makes me sound like an arm to a chair or something! I was named "Samantha Argorostis."

My father was first generation Greek American. He actually grew up with the one and only "Andrews" sisters! They're the three women that sang in most Abbott and Costello movies. Incredible! My roots, on my father's side, come from Thessaly, Greece. That is where the majestic Mount Olympus is. What a heritage! My mother came from German and other various assorted ethnicities. Irish, Dutch, and Scottish, also. I've also heard Native American. I'm not sure about that one! I can only recall what my little ears may have heard. Either way, I was never sure of the mixtures that my mother had. It could have been anyone's guess.

Basically, pick one! I grew up with an older sister and two brothers. At the time, my favorite was my little brother.

All six of us lived in a seventeen story building. Twelve buildings in total made up the "Smith" Projects. The complex was named after some man who was a Governor at one time. Alfred E. Smith. I'm a three year old child. Who is this Mr. Smith? How can one man build so many buildings?! This place was an entire world next to the East River and the Brooklyn Bridge. We had two bedrooms. One room was for us kids. It had two sets of bunk beds. I slept on one of the lower levels. I was too frightened to climb up to the top bunk, so it was the bottom for me! Although, I did worry about the upper bed falling on me one night while I would be asleep!

Well—the top bed never did fall! Screws held the beds and frame together. My father must have done a really good job putting the beds together!

Of course, we had our normal goodnight fights. "Mom! They're bothering me!" How many times my mother must have heard that! To this very day, I cannot imagine the patience my sister must have had. I suppose she slept through our whispering ranting! She must have been very brave to be in the same room with us! I would sometimes overhear conversations from my parents about a three bedroom apartment opening up. They agreed to stay right where they were. They wanted to keep the eat-in-kitchen and the view of the beautiful Church across the street. All of the stores were also across the street. We lived in the "first" building. Total convenience! We walked to everything in our world of The Smith.

I would think to myself "three bedrooms!" Oh, how great that would be! We wouldn't have to sleep on bunk beds, anymore! But we stayed right where we were.

I guess happiness was more important than the amount of bedrooms a family had. Besides, the three bedroom apartments were not in the "nice" people buildings. My parents, most undoubtedly, did the right thing.

Privacy was an issue, but we did deal with it pretty well. Somehow, my mother had bathroom schedules down pat! I think that she was more organized than she could have ever imagined!

Bathing Suits, Bubble Bath and Battleships

My mother believed in cleanliness. She also was the best water conserver on the planet! There was one bathroom, one bathtub, three small children, two boys and one tiny girl. I think back now and believe how much of a "psychologist" my mother was. Bath time! My mom would run the warm water as the liquid bubble bath magically created bubbles!

But my mother simplified awkwardness by telling us to put on our bathing suits! We, of course, had to share this little swimming pool with its sweet smelling bubbles. I guess it was smarter and easier this way, instead of my mother having to explain "why we should cover ourselves" in the bathtub. She made it fun! So naturally, we thought we were in a bubble pool. And we had on our bathing suits!

It was kind of like a day at the beach, without the sand.

My brothers and I got along well in the tub. But, it was not truly complete without the battleships. These were miniature aircraft carriers and they floated! I think every kid in the neighborhood had at least one battleship when they took their bath. It was probably a "must have" toy for the tub.

We had our battles in the bubbles in this little ocean. We enjoyed sinking each others battleship. After all, that's the fun part! What good is the purpose of a decent "boat" if you can't sink it? There were no rubber ducks for us! We were true warriors!

"It's time to get out!" My mother's brilliance—once again! Close the shower curtain and exit one at a time. Simplicity at its finest! She did this well and...we were clean for another day! We all smelled like sweet bubblegum, really! But for a kid, that's a good thing. Bubblegum is a fine invention. Every kid had to buy their Bazooka bubblegum. It meant nothing, though, if you couldn't blow bubbles properly. I, for one, was very good at this most fine talent! But when another child blew a large bubble, it was another kid's job to burst it! This obviously meant the gum blower had just gotten a smack on the mouth. Ouch! That's fun! I don't remember why my brothers and I "bickered." I only can think of how many times we all shared those words "Mom! He's bothering me!" Oh, yes! Of course the tables turned and one would hear "Mom! She's bothering me!" Then there was the combination of "Mom! They're bothering me!"

I had my name in there, too! After all, I was battling two brothers, two boys! Though, I had to be their match! So I had to be a "tough" little girl. Bedtime usually came after the bubble battle. Sweet dreams and nightmares. Typical kids hiding under the covers so that scary things wouldn't get them! Sometimes, I believe we might have actually said "goodnight" to one another. I can't recall if my older sister was there at "tuck in time." But if she was smart, she would have waited until we fell asleep. Then she could possibly "sneak" in and get some well deserved sleep.

New Jersey

I grew up with a hamster, a rabbit, a squirrel monkey and a most wonderful parrot that spoke to—me! We didn't have these animals all at the same time.

My father loved animals, I suppose. He worked as a bartender at a bar which resembled a jungle! It was owned by a nice man, who came to America from Africa. He had a daughter, and when my father sometimes brought me with him to work, she and I played together. I don't remember her name. She and I would feed the "bar cat" sliced ham after closing time. I was amazed at how much sliced ham a cat could eat! As for me, my favorite was bologna. So, the cat was most welcomed to the sliced ham! I know my father got the monkey and parrot from someone at the bar. Monkey's "do" really open refrigerators and throw eggs! I was always in trouble for releasing the monkey from his cage.

Mostly though, he let himself out! He was pretty smart. To my recollection, I got blamed, anyway. If an animal got loose, "Sam" did it! It is so hard to convince adults that you are totally innocent. So, sometimes children keep their mouths shut, not knowing if they will be believed. It is a big world for a child. They try so much to be truthful, but sometimes, the truth doesn't work. So they stay silent with a "funny" (really confused) look on their face. I had that "look" often!

The time would one day come when the monkey needed more space. My parents found a great "habitat" place called "New Jersey." So off he went! My parents told me that he now had plenty of space and he was very happy. And, I can honestly say that I know he was. Through my eyes, I thought this place must have been an animal Paradise! I pictured thick, green jungles and waterfalls! Then, it came time to let my parrot go to this most welcoming place in New Jersey. I missed her the most because she spoke to me. She would say my name. My mother told me that the parrot loved me the most. I always opened her cage! The rabbit was really my older brother's. He was great with her. I think that the rabbit was a "she." My little hamster, Sandy, was so smart! Even my mother would mention that scientists would say hamsters were not smart at all. We knew that they were wrong! My hamster would walk near the very edge of the kitchen table. She would look around, and then look downward. She turned around and didn't go to the edge again. Now, that was indeed intelligent!

I thought we could get these "scientists" to our apartment to see her. Then they might change their opinion. Yes, it was a fact, to me, that hamsters were very smart. Well, maybe only "my" hamster was smart! She was tiny, so I knew that she would not be going to live in New Jersey. She had a cage. But of course "the phantom animal cage opener" just couldn't resist letting her out to roam around the apartment. Sandy enjoyed her "freedom!"

One morning, I found her lying very still. I said her name. I touched her. She was very stiff. Her sweet, little tiny hands were folded as though they were in prayer. I knew that she was in Heaven. No New Jersey for her. I can remember burying her in the front grassy yard of the building that we lived in. I couldn't have been more than six years old, or so. I knew about death.

We also had little tiny water turtles. We took care of them so lovingly. Our turtles lasted much longer than all the other neighbors turtles. I guess it was "the thing" to have little turtles in apartments.

We bought the turtles from Chinatown. Almost anything can be purchased there. Really good stuff, too! Somehow, Salmonella wasn't rampant when I was a kid. My brothers and I would even kiss our turtles. We never got sick from any of our animal friends!

A dog or a cat was always totally out of the question! We didn't have the space and it also was not allowed in the Smith. My family, pretty much, went by the rules.

I, myself, had witnessed many times children lying. Simply telling a lie about...whatever they felt like lying about, I suppose. It did bother me. It upset me how kids could get away with telling lies! They even looked like they were telling the truth. How...strange. I was not much of a liar. I guess it comes "natural" to some kids. Then they grow up and live on lies all of their lives. What a useless word, "lie." It should be taken out of the dictionary. These were my thoughts.

Almost every year, for summer vacation, we went to New Jersey. Although, at the time, I don't believe that I knew that we were in New Jersey. I only knew it by the name of the town that we were in. I also knew it as the "country." Anywhere out of

Manhattan was considered the country. Maybe other places had more trees, or something. It wasn't a green forest that we went to. It was to a rented bungalow at the Northern Jersey Shore. It was at a beach! Sand pails and plastic shovels. What great inventions! There were many inventions as I was growing up. We'll come across them all, throughout my story. The sand was real hot! We needed to keep on our beach slippers. Otherwise, with each step, all that would be heard was "ouch, ouch, and more ouches!" The ocean's voice was the best part for me! The ocean was endless! My brothers and I had our brightly colored, brand new beach tubes. They were to keep us afloat. We really didn't need them. We were all great swimmers. No one taught us how to swim. We just swam. We swam within the murky, salty waters of New Jersey. It was nice being a fish for a while!

I suppose the beach tubes were a must have for children! The colors were cheerful and I really think parents felt better knowing that the tubes kept us safe, just in case. Then, beach hunger struck! My mother told us that the beach made you hungry. Oh, she was so right! Bologna sandwiches with sand! Our hands were covered with sand while we ate. We were hungry, so a little sand wasn't going to stop our mouths!

Then, there was the "Fudgy Wudgy" man. He sold chocolate ice cream on a stick. It was my father's job to get the ice cream. They were great! They were also mostly melted by the time they got into our little mouths.

Melted chocolate ice cream, sand, water! What else could there be?! The boardwalk! Oh, yes! Toys, fries, wooden floors and splinters! Keep on those beach slippers, whatever you do!

Behind our beach bungalow was a field. It looked more like a garbage dump! There was an old thrown away refrigerator. It still had its door attached. I guess, forty five years ago, there was no law to remove the doors on refrigerators that were disposed of. Well, there should have been a law. Two "neighbor" girls were back there. They told me that they were going to put me inside of the refrigerator and close the door!

I didn't know the word "murder." But they wanted to hurt me! That much I did understand. What a horrible thought to want to put anyone in a refrigerator! I was smart. I didn't come from the "country." I came from Manhattan! I stepped back and...ran! I was now in the safe haven of the rented bungalow with my family!

I think back on this and wonder if those girls knew of...death. If they had, would they still have tried to enclose me in that fridge of no way out? I don't know. I'm just glad that I ran! And...I was fast! I ran faster than boys! I had survived yet another day at the beach!

Raked!

I wasn't a nosey child. Adults frequently spoke in front of children. It seems the adults figured that children either didn't have ears or children didn't hear the bad things. I overheard some woman got...raked! I now know they said "raped." But I knew what a rake was. So that's what I

thought I heard them say. The maintenance men in "The Smith" kept the trees and grass in beautiful shape. I knew they used a rake to sweep the leaves when they fell off the trees in the Autumn. I pictured in my little mind a horrible scene! A man with a rake! How painful! A person being raked! The arms of a man ripping a woman apart with a rake! And the woman didn't die! I thought "What scars she must have!"

What terrible pain! I didn't want to think about how much blood there was. I never wanted to ever get...raked! The Smith was a huge place for a small child. A hard, sometimes mean, place to be. Especially, if you were a tiny little girl! People, in general, were more trusting back then. Or so it seemed. Mom would have me or my brothers cash in coca-cola bottles at the store. We would get two cents in return for these bottles. Mom would even give us money, dollars! She sent one of us to the store for milk, bread, cold cuts and cupcakes!

I would have the grocery list, and I would hand it to the "store" man. To my recollection, I might have been five years old. Every kid that had an apartment that faced the front of the building would be sent on this errand. This way, their mother could watch them from their window to make sure they were "safe."

But this time, I was going to a special store that was in the back of the building. Well, my mother couldn't see me back there! Along came two boys. I recognized one of them. I actually knew his name. I was little. They were a lot bigger than me. No one else was around. Just us…three! They stood in my way, and wouldn't let me pass. They both pulled down my "peddle pushers" (present day Capri pants) and I just stood there—frozen! I clutched tightly to the grocery list and the dollars. I had no pockets. I didn't yell. I couldn't seem to move my lips. I didn't know how they wanted to hurt me. But all the same, I "knew" they wanted to hurt me! Thank goodness for friends that face "the back" of the building! My neighbor, my friend, one whole year older than I was, yelled out of her window! "Leave her alone! Get your hands off of her!"

Then she came "downstairs" and chased them away! I was still standing there, frozen. She pulled up my pants and came to the store with me.

A child's memory can be sometimes unclear. I might have heard the word "rake," but I didn't see them holding any such thing. Thank the stars for other children's eyes! Thank the Heavens for friends. I will never forget her. I became "stronger" and so much "smarter" after that "near miss rake" incident.

Years later, when I was eight, another "attempt" was made by two other boys. In a building staircase, no less! I was eight, so I was bigger now. Or, so I thought. I kicked, I punched and yes, I ran like the wind! My friends were hanging out in the front of the building, so I was now safe!

I knew that I, for one, would not let anyone, ever again, try to "rake" me! Being a child, it's hard to tell parents of horrible incidents.

As a child, you don't know if they will believe you.

So I didn't tell my mother until I was an adult. Mom believed me. She was also...horrified! Back then, parents also allowed their children to go to the park. After all, it was right across the street. Everything was "across the street."

I went to the park. Maybe it was too early. I don't recall. My friends weren't there. I thought I would wait around and maybe they might show up to play on the swings. I was great on the swings. I would get up enough speed and hold on tight. Then I, swing and all, would go over the top bar and never once fall off! I was a little acrobat and I didn't even know it!

In the park that day, there was a little boy and a man. I had never seen them around before. I didn't know who they were. They were on the swings. The man was odd. I knew he meant me harm! No one ever taught me the word "kidnapped." But I did believe that this was his intention!

Both he and the little boy were calling me by the name Mary. They said that they wanted me to go home with them! I knew I had to "get away" from them! Thank goodness for torn fences! Yes! I got through a small opening in a fence and I ran across the street. I kept running, never looking back. I ran up four flights of stairs! I knocked on the door to our apartment, and I was let in to safety. I don't remember who opened the door. I don't even recall if I mentioned this to my mother. I only knew that I was safe now. No one here would call me "Mary."

This incident definitely made me a "smarter" person. Rather a smarter little girl, growing up in the City of New York. I would protect myself! I could always…run like the wind!

Gangs

Of course, being that there were twelve buildings in the Smith Projects, we only stayed with our "own" building friends. Each building's supposed "gang" was referred to by their building address number.

We lived in the first building. We were of the "good" building. There was also a private apartment complex across the street. They were the "true" enemies! We never carried any weapons, let alone even possess a key to our apartment door. Our "gang" consisted of girls that were between the ages of six and eight years old. But we did have our mouths! The tougher the voice, the better.

And we indeed were "tough"! No weapons. Just shouts of which gang could "rank" the best against the other. Our other defense mechanism was our eyes. We "rolled" our eyes. Dirty looks always prevailed! We had a lot of practice at this rolling of the eyes art. Simply, begin by closing your eye lids, slowly turn your head away. Flickering of the lids were the important factor here. And the bigger the eyes, the better!

We also "tisked". We made a tisking sound with our lips. This took practice! We were still young. In time, we would master this sound. But we still had our rolling eyes routine. And a most popular "ranking" term against the other was "Your mother!"

There would be a response of "Oh yeah! Your mother!"

This verbal war went on for a while. I really can't say, for sure, how long. Most likely, it took a matter of minutes. But to small girls, minutes are a long time! Which ever "gang" got the last tisk, word or dirty look in, was the winner of the "battle." The word "cool" wasn't used at that time in my life. The word "square" sometimes was. But, definitely the word tough! We were fantastic! We voiced without saying any "curse" words. What a victory! To use "curse" words made you bad! That's why we were from the "good" building. We fought our battles without saying one curse word. No punches were exchanged, either. Hey! We were kids!

Looking back, I have to say that we were definitely "cool!"

We were really good kids.

Melting Pot

I don't know who came up with this term. But I grew up with kids from many cultural backgrounds. We were all just kids.

We saw no "different" colors. We were all friends. If someone wanted to learn another language, other than English, all they had to do was visit the Lower East Side. A person could leave there with the education of a Linguist! The best place to be brought up "opened minded" is certainly,

without any doubt, a big city.

Segregation? This word was never in our vocabulary. It shouldn't be in anyone's. Sure, I would hear the phrase "stick to your own kind." My "own kind" were my friends! They were kids, so was...I. They, most certainly, were my own kind! We protected each other. We would listen to what the other had to say. We were there for one another. This was our own little "United Nations." Although, there were kids in the buildings "across the street." They would make remarks like "Go back to where you came from!" Well, I came from the good building. But I know what they meant. After the beach vacation and a hot summer, I was many shades darker than they were. So, I really knew what those other kids meant. And believe me—this was also my Country!

Yes, I knew of racism as a small child. Not in my household, but from other children. Perhaps they were taught this cruel word from their very own families! A person is a person. Either they are good or they are bad. That's what I was taught!

Skin color didn't matter. That much I did know. That much I did…believe.

In my "gang" we were smart, not closed minded, and most of all very brave! But we also knew not to walk to or go through certain neighborhoods. There we would most likely get hurt! So we mostly stayed in front of our building or the school park. What an environment to learn about life! I'm sure you get my drift!

There was only safety with friends or one's own family. Even neighbors were pretty great! There usually was an adult watching us, probably a mother or an older sister. I was far from being a teenager, yet I knew the world had some people that can be so cruel!

I knew what "danger" looked like. I saw "innocent" faces try to hurt me, try to take me away! But I was able to observe. The concept of having "logic" at a very young age is very rare. But I felt that if I feel safe, then I most likely am safe. Safety had to be fought for! When you are under eight years old, you fight with your mind—With your own logic. Feeling harm or feeling safety. Either way, your survival in a large city had to be fought for. And having just two eyes wasn't enough!

Since our apartment window faced the front of the building, I had a great advantage! If I felt any harm approaching me, all I had to do was yell "Mom! Mommy! Mom!" My mother was quick! She'd be at the window in a flash! "Is someone bothering you?!" If I was being bothered, I had my mother to make sure I would get to my apartment safely. She would wait for me in the hallway. I would hear her voice call to me and I ran to her! Home! Safety...!

Shoelaces

Before entering Kindergarten, every child should know how to tie their own shoes. Our shoes and sneakers had shoelaces in them. There was not any type of self-closures for sneakers or shoes. I think back to my mother's genius mind! My mother organized a shoelace tying legacy. My sister taught my older brother how to tie his laces. He, in turn, taught me. I taught my little brother. My younger brother got away easy! He didn't have to teach anyone how to tie their shoe laces! There were no more children left, after him, to teach. Sometimes, I guess, it might be great being the youngest one! Myself, my sister and my brothers were definitely professionals in the art of tying shoe laces! But my sister was the expert at baby tooth pulling. Yes! String tied to a doorknob. The other end tied around that loose tooth. And…get ready! Slam the door! The tooth came out perfectly! There was no injury to the patient. Just a monetary reward from that nice tooth fairy! I had a most talented family. We were jacks of all trades. I, for one, was great at hiding and doing the crying game. I don't remember why. It was mostly when we had "company."

Now that I think about it, I cried because I didn't want to eat. The roast was always mostly undercooked. It bothered me to see the blood oozing out from it! My mother was so smart, though. Mom got me to eat. She would thinly slice the roast and fry it to a crisp! Then I ate it. It was hard to chew, but it was cooked!

My family wasn't perfect. Not anywhere near it, I guess. But give us some multi-colored clay and our imaginations went into a complete symphony! Dinosaurs and dino eggs were our specialty! My big brother made the best clay sculptures. He definitely inherited my father's hand for creating art work! I was second best. So I suppose my little brother came in third at clay sculpturing. Maybe it's not so easy being the youngest, after all!

We got along good at playtime. I believe problems arose at the dinner table. I remember hurting my big brother with a fork on his hand. I cannot, for the life of me, remember why I hurt him. I know it's about forty something years later, but bro—if you are reading this—"I am so, so sorry!" My mother was also way ahead of everything. She (and possibly the entire family) had to eventually teach me and my brothers how to write our names. If it weren't for my mom's brilliant thinking—I'd be going through life with the name "Sam Arg!" It would have been much easier on us three if we had shorter names, such as: Chan or Jones. My mom taught real well, but my good memory helped me out...a lot!

Scary Things

I received a Christmas present from Santa Claus. I always wondered why on earth Santa would want to give me the creeps. He gave me a doll that was taller than I was! She also stared at me. I would have nightmares about her! "She" can be compared to "Chucky." But back then, it was quite scary to have a doll that was bigger than I was. I am so glad that she didn't talk! On top of things, I had to carry her around. I was a little bit of a thing, carrying a doll that was bigger than I was. She could hardly even bend. She was not soft and cuddly. She just constantly kept her eyes wide open and they were looking at...me!

Whatever became of her, I don't even want to know. Maybe—my parents sent her to that wonderful animal place in New Jersey. For the animal's sake, I hope that they didn't! We had, of course, a small black and white television set. For some unknown reason, it was built into a huge, wooden box. "The Beast from 20,000 Fathoms!" This movie was one of the scariest because the monster came out of the East River. This particular river was right down the street from where I lived! These nightmares were worst than my big doll nightmares. A little child running from a dinosaur! Dream solution: Climb up building! It's amazing how a child can guide themselves out of danger in their nightmares!

The other scariest movie of all time, to me, was "The Thing." He also stalked me in my nightmares! I'd hide up on a chandelier, so he couldn't find me. We didn't even have a chandelier. But in my dreams, I was up there. He never did get me!

I mostly enjoyed watching scary movies with my father. I know he made the movies scarier than they were. "He's gonna get you!" My response was always "Aaahhh!"

I was scared but I knew my father was there and he'd protect me from those monsters. It's too bad that my father couldn't be in my nightmares. I know he would have gotten rid of the monsters and they would never have tried to get me again! We were lucky if we even received four channels! Our living room television had "rabbit ears." Every family that was fortunate of having a T.V. had their good old antenna right on top of the wood box.

Mostly, the picture went up and down. Sideways, too! Wiggly, and then wigglier. This way; that way. "Mom! The T.V.'s going up and down, again!"

My father had already made new "ears" for the antenna, since the ones that it had were bent at least a thousand times. Wire hangers! Good invention. But, aluminum foil has hangers beat by a mile! "Tin" foil! Definitely a great invention! Wonderful sheets of thin, flexible metal on a roll in a box. And the box had its very own cutting teeth when you were ready to cut a piece off! The box housed what my mother would "mechanically" attach to the wire hanger ears.

The box was dangerous. It can also be considered a "scary" thing. Not a good invention!

No matter how careful one was, they got cut by the hard teeth of the box. But it was all worth it. Television was saved by my mother! We only got around 4 fuzzy channels, but we didn't mind!

When mom got too busy, my brothers and I took turns being the antenna. One of us held it until the station was clearer. The drawback to this was whomever was the "antenna," had to stay still. Watching T.V. bent over in a truly almost impossible position, holding what used to resemble an antenna. Now, that was hard work. The remote control and cable T.V. were invented many, many and many years too late! These inventions would have given my mother a little more leisure time and a lot less work. But I never heard her complain, not even once.

I clearly remember my older brother and I saw a giant bee outside of the living room window. It hovered and looked at us. It was about one foot in length! I wonder if my brother remembers that. Maybe, one day I'll ask him. I also know that I saw the "crawling hand." I did! It was outside our building near one of the stairwell entry doors. It was! I know I saw it! It was crawling, just like in the movie. I ran into the elevator and went home! "Mom! I just saw the crawling hand downstairs!"

I can't recall if she even responded. My mother probably thought that I shouldn't be watching those scary movies, so much, with my father. My father might have even gotten blamed!

My mom was probably right! I watched too many scary movies. (But I know what I saw!)

My mother had a big heart. She would give derelict men, also referred to as "Bowery Bums," a plate of food. Usually, they would come, one at a time. This was all taking place in the staircase hallway in the building.

My mother would later find the food and plate had been thrown! She would clean it up and say that the man probably wanted money for liquor. My mom was most likely right. She was so trusting and very giving. I learned a lot about people, in general, at such a young age. My mother was a great cook. The "bum" was missing out on a really delicious, home cooked meal! My sister and brothers can vouch for me that it was indeed a fact that my mother was an excellent cook. I can also vaguely remember my mother's conversations with other mothers. Most likely neighbors. I would stand next to my mother and wait very patiently, while she and another mother had an "unclear" conversation. Well, it was unclear to me! I do believe that my mother actually invented a word. I say this because I have never heard it come out of anyone else's mouth. I will put this "invented word" into a sentence of a mother's conversation. My mom: "You know. Whatchamacallit!"

The response from other mother: "Oh, yeah. I know. What's her name?! You know! That one!" The person being described as "Whatchamacallit" could be narrowed down by the floor they lived on. Better yet, by their apartment number!

Neither one of them remembered the name; hut the apartment number was most helpful. At least now they both knew, more or less, about whom they were referring to. "Oh, yeah. Her!" This most unusual (invented by my mother) word was also used in a telephone conversation. I always would wonder what the other person on the other end of the telephone was thinking. Did they truly understand who "Whatchamacallit" was? Perhaps, they did indeed. It easily flowed out of my mother's mouth. Definitely a most unique word, a one of a kind invention! I might have heard it spoken from one other person in my entire life. My older sister. I do believe that she might still use the word.

This word could also describe other "things", such as a place, a man, and an instrument—maybe a tool. It was a very versatile word. And—it solely belonged to my mother!

Throughout my story, I would like to focus on the ages of three to eight and three-fourths. My memory begins from three years old and on. I don't want to include my teenage years. I don't think anyone would want to hear about my very first "training" bra. This, by the way, had to be invented by someone who never wore one! Two words for a bra:

Total Discomfort. And I won't get into my very first period, either. No one wants to hear about my first sanitary napkin! There should be a warning label on the package on this horrid invention! WARNING: Welcome to hell! You are now a teenager. Must use silver colored safety pins that might open when you sit down. (Attach pins to napkin and underwear.) I ask—"Who the heck invented these?!" Nope! I won't get into my teen years. I'll keep it simple.

Block Parties

There were always yearly "Block Parties." The term "block" was actually a New York City form of mathematics! For example, one street equaled one block. For one, The San Gennaro Feast! This was held in Chinatown. From my building it was across the street, one block, and then across a really big street with lots of cars. Then finally—one more block!

Children couldn't make this dangerous feat alone! Parents and an older sister came in very handy. They were great at tackling the cars which came from different directions. This "Feast" was best at night. It had the very best, yes—fireworks!

What visions to capture in total half shock, due to the loud sonic booms! Fireworks just wouldn't be the same without the heart stopping noise. The rockets whistled to the sky. And believe me, there were a lot of booms! The great thing about the fireworks were all of the beautiful colors as they exploded! I was always left with whitish spots before my eyes. Blurry spots that weren't pretty. The Feast men held a large statue of a Saint. Lots of money hung all over the statue—dollars! Billions of dollars, too! This, I was told, would go to a church. Nope. I think it went to those men holding the heavy Saint. I could be right, you know?

Where else could a child see a doll head on a long stick?

Here! Right here at an Italian Feast in Chinatown. That's where! A stick, and on the top of it was a doll's head! A piece of lace imitated a dress. Very strange. A doll with only a head! Yes, strange. But I just had to have one! Italian sausages and some fried doe with powdered sugar could be smelled all around!

I think adults went there just to smell stuff. Kids enjoyed the little games, like trying to fill up a balloon with water. A water gun aimed at a balloon which was never in shooting distance for anyone! If anyone was lucky enough to get the water inside the balloon to burst it, they would get a prize. The prize was never the large teddy bear that sat on a top shelf. Nope! They got some little rubber lizard or even a key chain which resembled a skeleton. What does a key chain made of fake bones have to do with a Saint?!

These are not very good prizes. I'll stay with my bodiless doll on a stick!

Across the street, make a left and yet, a school yard "party"! This was a day time venture for children. Some adults were with us kids. The party was for the adults at night time. This party had music. It was called "Latin" music. It truly sounded nothing like a Priest's language, while speaking at mass at a church. This music had a great beat! Everybody danced! I also think that there was food being sold.

I would not stay long, though. It was probably a block party for the adults, anyway. But the dancers were the best, ever!

Twirling, feet moving in beat to the music! Now, these were real dancers! They were also neighborhood people that lived in The Smith! I knew, one day, I too would dance like that! However, the best "real" block party came to us. It was right at the street in the front of the entire building! Police must have thought it was an important block party. They closed off the street that led into the block. They would use their police cars and park them sideways so that no other cars could get in.

There were little rides just for kids! Ohhh! And this was a true party! Even the "bad building people" were there. Everyone was welcomed. There was food, too. I don't remember what they had to eat. But it had to be something really good.

Each little ride had its own music. Everyone was safe there. Especially, with the police hanging out! They ate and enjoyed talking to everyone. Now—this was a true street party. And it was taking place on the entire block in front of my building! There may not have been a beach there, or a boardwalk. But it was great, anyway!

I might have seen a doll head on a stick there, too. Maybe I didn't. Either way, these were great outdoor parties! They might have sold balloons. If they did, my brothers and I went home with a balloon. I can't remember clearly. I must have been real young. Probably even an age without the added half to it!

Easy to get home, too. Just go across the street!

They might be hard to blow up, but balloons rate high on my great invention list! The ones at the block party were blown with a machine! This was the best part of this party. Watching, trying to be patient, as a piece of colorful rubber turned into a balloon. Oh, and don't ever let go of it. It could fly away, way up to the stars! It could! I saw some actually do it. The kids that had this happen to their balloons cried. My balloon didn't get away. If it had, I would have cried, too. After all, kids make the most unusual sounds when they cry. Kids cry the best!

In my family, I could "out cry" my brothers. Amazing how tears stop instantly when I would be given ice cream or a candy bar! Hey. Kids cry. Reason: Because they can! Kids laugh a lot, too! So do adults. Laughter rates above crying any day! And you don't need a tissue to blow your nose either, like when you're crying. Then lots of tissues are needed!

My brothers and I weren't "wanters." For example, we never, ever ranted or raved and said "I want that!" I heard other children do this pounding of the hands and feet "want dance."

We were better mannered, I suppose. Or, maybe we weren't "wanters" because our parents already knew what we "wanted." This is a huge difference. Wanting something or asking politely. Even shyly, was certainly not being a "wanter."

These "neighborhood" block parties brought to children good dreams. No monster was going to be chasing me after being with firecrackers and balloons! Although, where's that doll on a stick with no body?! Hmmm.

There were also parades! I'm sure there were many. I only remember one, "The Veteran's Parade!" Or, to a child's ears, "Vet-trains." My father would put on his old "Air—Corps" hat from World War II and proudly march with other Vet-trains!

There were never children or women in these parades. Only soldiers. And a huge American Flag. Anyone in a uniform was such a proud sight to see. It seemed to be a sign of respect. I wasn't sure as to why is was, I only knew that my father stood with his head up high as he marched!

There might have been a drum band, too. Or, I think there was.

This would bring me back to thinking about the most asked question of teachers. "What do you want to be when you grow up?" I thought maybe I could be a soldier, too! But I mustn't tell anyone— because that's for boys. My father was a Bombardier. He never spoke about the war. But he was good at watching those war movies!

My father had a picture of himself and the actor Gig Young wearing soldier uniforms. My dad fought in the war with this tall actor. My father always watched Gig Young's movies. I might have, too. After all, he was my father's friend!

My father used to play with Leo Gorcey when they

were kids. A talent scout picked him, instead of my dad, to be in movies. Maybe the talent scout thought that my dad was too handsome! "The Bowery Boys" and "The East Side Kids." I remember.

I've always had a great memory!

Church

Going to church was a must! Otherwise, it was a sin if you didn't go!

I mostly went, yes—across the street to the beautiful Catholic Church. Now and then, I would visit the Greek Orthodox Church which was in Chinatown. I would go with my father. He was Greek Orthodox. My mother was Catholic.

One of the worst sins for a child was to actually say the "S" word. Not like "Oh. No! I stepped in dog stuff." But the real word for the dog's stuff... The "S" stuff!

I wasn't introduced to the "F" word. So, pretty much, I was in the clear. I never had too much to confess at church. I may have come close to wanting to say the "S" word. Sometimes, I'd have to try to make up sins! For instance, jay-walking against the red light. Or even better yet (to a Priest anyway), I thought about punching my brother. Hey. As long as the Priest was pleased to give me my repeated prayer punishment, I was okay. My worst confession was playing with a girl who was one whole year older than me! She actually said the entire "S" word! And she wasn't sorry. I told my mother. My mother brought me to the girl's apartment and she told her mother. In turn, an entire denial argument commenced. This girl tried to make both of our parents believe that I said the "S" word! My mother believed me! She heard this girl say words that were "inappropriate" all of the time. It's good news to a child when they are believed by their mother!

Normally, adults seem to believe the first child that speaks.

Kind of like first come, first served. Like an Automat. You know! It's a restaurant where a person would put a quarter into a machine and they would get a hot bowl of macaroni and cheese. What a good idea! Well, I liked the way it tasted!

A most challenging word is the simple word "ask." If you grew up in New York City it was pronounced "ax." Ohhh, yes it was!

To this very day, you can't take my accent away. And I've lived in another State and other areas. There's nothing better than a Manhattan accent.

It's just so...real!

In a church it was thoughtful to light white candles. But there was a catch! You had to leave change in the candle box. I would give what I could afford. But I was with other girls that gave nothing! To me this was a terrible sin! They lit candles for free. Yes!

That's a sin, alright! I don't even think that they lit them for anyone special. I don't think that they even prayed when they lit these stolen "lights."

These girls were also notorious for "stealing" Barbie doll clothes.

I never did. I knew it was wrong. So they didn't want to play with me, anymore. I tried to tell my mother that they were thieves! They never confessed this, either.

I wasn't going to be "pressured" into stealing because kids said "do it!" Nope! I had a strong mind. I knew that it was wrong.

I certainly knew wrong from right! And I didn't want to be in jail at eight and a half years old! They were a whole year older than I was. I wondered "Is this how it is to be nine years old?"

Within this beautiful church was a most magnificent ceiling painting of Jesus. His eyes were always looking into mine. His eyes were so very...sad. He was beautiful! But I always thought that his mother was wonderful! Saint Mary. As a child, she was always there for me.

My parents had a beautiful statue of Saint Mary enclosed in a glass case. She was so beautiful!

Praying to her was much nicer than being in church. We were alone. I could tell her my dreams, my thoughts. I knew that she was listening to me.

Her statue now sits in my bedroom. A last gift to me from my mother. I cherish the statue. I believe it was my grandmother's.

I never met my grandparents on either side of my family. I wasn't born yet when they passed away. I always wondered what it would have been like to have a Grandma and a Grandpa. I'll never know the answer to this.

I'll tell you a secret. I still pray to the statue of Saint Mary, all alone, when I'm in my bedroom. I know that she still hears me.

When church mass was over, I would hear children and people saying the worst things when we got outside! Cursing, gossip, even perhaps—lies! Such awful things said right after being in church! I was well ahead on the road to learning how people can be.

The doors to the churches were never locked. If

someone needed extra comfort, they were welcomed to visit within at any time.

So much trust has been misplaced in the world—by us!

I always wore a little white head veil while others wore a tissue with a bobby pin. I wasn't sure if this is what the church truly meant by "covering your head."

End of Summer

I enjoyed the end of summer. It would soon be "new clothing and shoes" shopping time! My sister brought me shopping. We'd take a bus to May's and Klein's on 14th Street. The bus "ride" was like going on a far off journey! But I was not alone. I had my big sister with me for this great bus trip!

While entering the stores I would realize we would be there forever. To a child forever is a few hours. It seemed like...days! But my sister would get great things for me! New great things! Not any "hand me downs" for me! But why is it children never say that their shoes are too tight? I grew within a year. I wear a half size bigger, now! I said absolutely nothing.

A child really thinks they're being, I guess, bad if they complain. A very simple "I need a bigger size" would have been helpful to me if I had spoken up.

Though—I was the one that wore tight shoes throughout the entire school year! I should have told her they "hurt." My sister's the one that taught me how to shop and get things "on sale" at half the price! What a concept. I could get two of whatever it was that was on sale!

What I missed about summer was "vacation." Family vacations! They are the best things in life that a family can do together. Family is great! Family is love. Family, to me—was safety. Friends are great. I think when you are a child friends are much more important. If a child only knew how really important their family could be. When they grow up, sometimes they learn this value.

There's nothing like taking a break from shopping. An eating break!

New York City pizza has and always will be the very best pizza on the entire planet! A slice of pizza eaten the way pizza should be eaten! Folded and with your two hands. Crispy crust that stays folded, creating easy access to the mouth. Real pizza, flipped up into the air then placed into the hottest oven that was ever made! Another "great" (and delicious) invention, New York City pizza!

Well, some more clothes shopping to do. Off to yet another store!

My little legs are getting real tired. In fact, my entire self is getting real tired.

I asked (axed) my sister "Can we go home now?"

Her response was "Okay, but we have to go to the second floor."

I guess it will be a few more hours (days) than I thought.

I'm practically falling asleep while standing up.

"Please. Can we go home now?"

Waiting for the bus to get home was quite aggravating. Most likely, the wrong bus always came way ahead of "your" bus.

Finally, our bus! Nope! Not the right bus. Some more waiting, and then—yes! I know this has to be our bus!

Now we're on our way home. Yes, home! T.V. and snacks!

Most importantly, a bathroom where no one can peek!

I'd plead to my mother "Can I try the clothes on tomorrow?"

My mother would say "You have to try them on today. If they don't fit, we'll have to go back to the store(s)."

I'm exhausted! I can pass on the bubble bath tonight!

Ah, yes! Tomorrow will be my big brother's turn to go shopping!

First Fist Fight!

At age eight, I wasn't familiar with the "F" word. But another "F" word, most definitely! "Fight!" Fist fight, no less. I got picked on when I came out of church, wearing my "communion" white dress.

A boy hit me first! He made fun of me for wearing a dress, no less. I held my tears in; my lip was bleeding, and then wham! I knocked him down to the ground! My very first victory! In fact, my very first fist fight and it was with a boy.

I never started a fight. Fists came to me—Directly to my face! I knew I had to learn how to "duck!" "Ducking" I would master. King Alexander the Great was alive, living in a little girl's eight year old body. And "he" was wearing a dirty, torn (once white) dress!

Well, my brilliant mother rescued the dress. She dyed it blue. Dye, another good invention! Needle and thread was a better invention! Band aids—a must have item in every household where I grew up! But that "red" stuff in a bottle was really painful! I preferred peroxide. I liked watching the white bubbles form as the cut, (especially on the knee) soaked it up. Peroxide also was not as painful as the red stuff!

I'll never know if my mother believed that I hadn't started the fight. Never the less—a very good, though painful, learning experience! I wasn't pain resistant. I probably cried alone in the bathroom, but maybe I don't want to remember that!

Tears were for sissies. I wasn't going to he called a sissy, ever! In my pre-teen and teen years, I got picked on by girls. Most of the time, the reason was because I gave them a "dirty" look. Or, I rolled my eyes at them. Rolling one's eyes was a definite art form. I did this form of art very well!

Either way, they were only using an excuse to fight. Some girls were that way where I lived. But they were from another building. They were "the bad building" girls! They were also liars.

But I would like to stick to my three to eight years old childhood memories!

They were the most adventurous compared to my teen years. My sister was ten years older than me. I suppose she did her homework on her own. My brothers and I did ours together. The kitchen table was the most popular meeting place in the apartment. Mostly everything was right there in the kitchen! And it had two windows that faced different directions. We could overhear gossip. We had ring side seats watching other people argue outside! What a view! Many things to witness from a kitchen window, without stepping one foot outside!

Boys

Growing up, when a boy liked you, why is it that he had to hit you? I'll probably never know the answer to that question.

Though, I could guess. Perhaps, it had to do with embarrassment.

(Hey, I just realized that the word "ass" is in that word!)

That was big me talking, not little me.

Whatever the reason, that's how I learned how to really fight.

I defended myself well. I fought like a boy! I didn't scream and I didn't do any "hair" pulling, either. That's what girls do. And I was fighting a boy. I boxed! I had to. If I hadn't I'd get beaten to a pulp!

So I learned quickly! I kicked many a boy's butt, for sure.

I guess a lot of boys liked me. Hey! That's how it was. I had no choice. I had to fight back. The worst threat was "I'll meet you outside at three o'clock"! Oh no! I dreaded the three o'clock school bell. End of the school day!

A bully (boy) would be waiting in the school yard. He was waiting for...me! There was no grass. There was concrete. If we got lucky, there was blacktop. It's not as painful as being thrown down on concrete!

I was afraid, but I didn't show it. I fought back. I won!

One boy actually "chickened" out on me. I did give the most serious "dirty looks!"

I figured if I wanted to go home, have a snack and do homework, I would have to beat this boy up real fast!

I got home in plenty of time to watch our wiggly pictured T.V. And with time to spare for my bathing suit, bubble bath and battleships! Then, goodnight! Straight, uninterrupted sleep, and of course I did my homework first.

I'd awake to cornflakes with bananas, bacon or oatmeal. I loved oatmeal. I coated it with more sugar than there was oatmeal in my dish!

My friends would pick me up and we'd walk to school. After all, it was (yes)—across the street! School was at the beginning of Chinatown. Public

School # 1. That made us girls feel great, our school was number "one!"

On the short walk to school, we would hope that a boy didn't like us that week! A little girl can get tired of fighting with a boy. But you're not allowed to say enough is enough! That wasn't a concept back then. Lump it or leave it was what it was! However that phrase may have related to anything, that's how it was.

At that young age, I can never remember any teachers breaking up a fight after the three o'clock bell rang.

They broke up the lunch time fights. I think that they liked the three o'clock bell to ring, so that they could get out of there! The really could have been some kind of supervision. We had no "monitors," no school nurse, no three o'clock guards. We had a crossing guard. But she wasn't in the school yard. At P.S. #1, the Principal played the part of the nurse, guidance counselor and whatever role he may have had to fit into. There were grades K through sixth grade. We were not...protected!

Christmas

Snow was a real treat for children living in the City! We didn't get snow very often. But when we did, it was snow ball fight time!

The snow never lasted very long. It would also get very dirty with all the cars that drove through it. When the snow would first arrive, it was a child's wonderment! Christmas time was great in our apartment!

My father would "lug" home the biggest, real Christmas tree! We didn't have a car. I never knew how he got it home. But every year he did! It smelled delightful!

My father stenciled the window panes with snowflakes by spraying "snow in a can." It looked so real. It was great! My parents used a razor blade, after the holiday, scraping it off of the windows. It took hours! I was glad that it wasn't my chore, especially since I wasn't allowed to use a razor or any other sharp object—for that matter. Under the tree were the most pretty gift boxes. Within them were fantastic toys! Before Christmas came, my sister, me and my brothers would always get a brand new, crisp one hundred dollar bill! This amazing gift was from our parents!

There was one for each of us four children. One hundred dollars, forty something years ago, was a great deal of money! Even today it's a lot of money!

My father was no longer a bartender. He was now a bank advertiser. He was great making up ads for the bank that he worked for. Do you remember "The And-Car Loan?" He created that idea!

My father must have cashed a lot of checks at the bank that he worked at to get those great, clean one hundred dollar bills!

I spent my money real fast! I first bought gifts for friends.

Then I bought cheaper gifts for my family. Most of the money went on me. I was a little girl! What else would a small child do with a great deal of money? I could have spent every dollar

of it on just myself. Well, I kind of did. That's not the point. I wasn't really selfish... Maybe just a little bit.

It was all mine and I spent it. So there!

I think we took more pictures of the Christmas dinner than of all of us. Perfectly done roasted turkey! It always looked so familiar. Ah, yes. It resembled the Thanksgiving turkey and all of its pictures, too!

Why is it that there is never enough stuffing? It's almost a wonder of science itself. More stuffing goes into the oven than what comes out of it. It's a never ending mystery!

Then the "company" showed up! There were adults, other kids, and people I didn't recognize. Were they cousins?!

One boy, a year younger than I was, called me a sissy. Well, I let him have it! I didn't punch him. This was not my real first fight. I pushed him against my huge, beautiful metal doll house that my father had put together for me. The boy fell on it and it could not be fixed! I felt it was worth it. He cried and never called me that name again!

I did miss the doll house, though. It had a blue door and a door bell with lights that worked! I must say—I did a really good job setting him straight! I was even madder now! I no longer had my doll house. He really better keep away from me!

My favorite Aunt was the best visitor! Aunt Margie was not "company." She was...family! She was my mother's older sister. She made me feel so cozy when she stayed a week or so. She wasn't married and she had no children. I loved her visits. She was so tiny. She reminded me of a little kitten. Not with claws, she was just so cute. She smiled a lot and said "Hi, ya!" Aunt Margie gave the best "eye-winks!" She rode the train from uptown Manhattan. Then she would walk from the train to our apartment. Her neighborhood was clean and safe back then. It's changed a lot. Horribly a lot!

We would always have Christmas gifts under the tree just waiting to be opened by my Aunt! I also believed that my mother and father gave her money. She needed it. That's what I was told, anyway. Boys never seem to like clothing for gifts, no less for Christmas gifts. On the other hand, I loved getting clothes for Christmas. I loved getting clothes for any occasion. If they are gifts, I don't have to spend long hours (days) at clothing stores! Nothing ever had to be brought back to the store for an exchange. Every thing was usually big on me. My mother solved this problem. She was great with a needle and thread! Almost everything I had to wear got hemmed. Mom was also a wizard with a sewing machine! I also got pretty girl stuff from those pretty wrapped boxes from under that big tree.

It might have been everyone's job taking off the decorations. I'm really not sure. But when it was gone, the living room just wasn't the same. The tree was real! Maybe we can keep it and just water it everyday. That would have been a good idea, (I guess.)

Noises

I slept to the true sounds of "creatures of the night!" I don't know if I could have fallen asleep without the noises. And there were many of a variety of noises. Thank goodness they came from "outside!"

Gunshots were most common. At three a.m. there were sounds of police sirens, people just hanging out, and neighbors arguing!

In New York City one cannot have a good night's sleep without the noises! If a person grew up with these sounds it was easy to fall asleep. But if you just so happen to move there, and "think" that you are a New Yorker, you're not about to get any sleep! It's really something that you have to be "born" into. With patience, you might get used to it. I knew when I was under the covers, things were just fine! We had great neighbors that lived on our floor. If they borrowed a cup or a pot, when they returned them, they weren't empty. There was sugar in the cup, and a home made, hot dinner in the pot. Nice neighbors! I can add "incinerators" to my great, yet dangerous, invention list. These were very noisy! But it was the only way to get rid of garbage. It had a small door with a handle. To open it, grab the handle and pull downward. Hope that the fire doesn't happen to come blazing up once you have the door open! The contents thrown inside would get burned. But first you had to slam the door shut! Open it again, slam it again. Open it, and then peek inside. Job accomplished! All of the garbage got down with only two tries!

When I ate something that I didn't like, guess where it went? Not the garbage. It could be found there! Advice: Leave no proof.

The incinerator! Throw item in, close door, all gone! Nope. I was very brave. To get this unwanted meal down, I would have to "slam" the door! Someone might hear. I might get caught throwing food away. I slowly opened the incinerator door and I put my hand inside! I felt greasy stuff! That wasn't what I put inside. I must find my morsel quickly and "throw" it down! This kind of looks like what I originally put inside. Got it! And I left no evidence! But now I have to wash off the slimy stuff that is now all over my right hand and arm! The incinerator did come in handy, but after having to put my hand and arm in—I don't know if I'll keep it on my list of good inventions! The most aggravating noise was when people had outside conversations. I'm talking about the middle of the night! One person would be yelling out of their window! They had to shout so that the person "downstairs" would hear them! I knew about telephones. I thought they just didn't have one. People were having conversations without even picking up a telephone. Amazing! Where else can an accomplishment like this be done?

There was always "the good Samaritan" that yelled at the two of them. "Shut up! People are trying to sleep!" Of course, they would yell right back at this person. Then it became a three person "conversation!" (Hey, thanks a lot, Mister!) Then there might be barking from mysterious dogs. They were not allowed here. People knew that. Now the dogs were having a barking conversation! Remedy: Put covers over head.

In "the bunk bed" room, there was a white "princess" rotary telephone. I always liked the color pink. I thought that the telephone would look nice in pink. Umm? Yes, my sister's nail polish! That'll do it!

So with a small bottle of nail polish, I painted away!

It upset my mother. She said we didn't own the telephone. It belonged to the telephone company and that we were renting it.

My mother's toiling, time consuming remedy was nail polish...remover! Lots of it, too! It must have taken her hours upon hours to undo my artwork. I didn't think it was anywhere near funny. I felt really bad. I thought that she would be happy.

I did do a real good job. I just had this urge to paint things, like my father's hand made, wooden bar. I got my hands on a can of clear, shiny stuff. "Varnish" is what it was called. All that I needed now was a paint brush. I really thought my father would like the bar shinier with a much darker color. Oh, boy!

Nail polish remover wasn't going to "fix" this one!

I knew that I was going to be watching war movies for a long time.

Material was another superb invention! Thumb tacks and leopard fur (hopefully fake) began to take shape around the bar. My father was good at this. I wasn't allowed to help. I can't say that I blame my dad. I didn't know why he hadn't liked my idea in the first place!

I'm sure there was plenty of "verbal noise" for that one!

I don't remember. I just felt bad that I did something that made my father very unhappy. Not to mention my mother, too!

Maybe they won't get mad at me if I have fun melting crayons on the hot radiator. Wrong, again!

My parents should have considered that I possibly needed a canvas and some real paint.

My creative "talent" was never expanded upon!

So I went to crayons and paper. I was pretty good at this.

And my parents were not getting mad at me, either!

It wasn't as much fun as my previous artwork, but I had never "painted" any furnishings again.

I, personally, thought I had done a great job. I might have one day become "The nail polish painting Queen!"

Such a great talent was being wasted!

Although, one thing for certain, I was a very honest child.

I took my blame. I never denied my "doings." I also never tried to put the blame on anyone else. I wouldn't have been "me" if I...lied.

Besides, I took a lot of "pride" in my artwork. I

wasn't going to give the "credit" to anyone else!

Believe me when I say that when I made trouble, it was for Myself! I took total responsibility for all of my actions, even if I didn't think they were wrong.

One day, we were sent home early from school. That day, there were no noises. There was silence. I was eight years old.

President John F. Kennedy was killed.

On that day, there were silent tears...

The Front

Parents didn't have to escort their children to play outside. There was no need to. After all, everyone had their great windows! Cars would be parked on the street near the sidewalk of the front of our building. Car hoods were a good place to rest when we got tired. Good old parked cars! A bunch of kids could play for hours, as long as we stayed "in front" of the building. We had to be in view of our parent's eyes at all times.

I couldn't have been more than six years old, well, maybe seven. It just was not allowed for any of the kids to drift away from the unseen eyes that lurked from all of those windows. We were being…watched!

Rubber bands are most amazing, another great invention! They could skillfully be tied together to create a "Chinese jump rope!" It would be held at either ends. Only the best could master turning it around their feet, hands and jumping over it without touching it. What a fun game, and all this from only using rubber bands! I was excellent at this rubber band "gymnastics!" I was indeed the Chinese jump rope master! We also had "regular" jump rope. A simple rope also held at either ends. Not touching the rope was the true goal and also jumping over it!

"Double Dutch" with two ropes was the ultimate challenge. I was also the Double Dutch master! We also sang songs to the rhythm of the ropes snapping on the concrete. A most fantastic snapping sound to a little girl's ears!

I could have possibly been in a jump rope Olympics! Unfortunately, I hadn't heard about any such "sport" at the time.

Rabbit foot key chains were "the thing" every child had to have. We didn't have any keys to put on them. We just carried them around. I always pictured a lot of bunnies hopping around on three feet. But everyone had to have a rabbit foot. They were for good luck! How on earth can anyone get good luck when the rabbit is missing a foot?! Magic? I didn't know. But it was a necessity. Poor rabbits, though.

It was so incredible to find so much, either across the street or right there at "the front" of the building!

Fire hydrants to us were instant hot summer beaches, of course, without the sand. It was our very own flowing ocean. The Firemen would come along and actually open up the fire hydrant for us children. They used a large wrench. Sometimes, it took two of these big men to open just one!

Water would gush out for what seemed like hours! We even had our beach balls with us!

All of this, right there. The front was great! When hunger struck, the candy store harbored every single candy known to humankind! A penny a piece, and of course the candy store was called "The penny candy store." Good hint! Tiny peanut better cups were my favorite! Although, a child had to always share. I would gobble up as many as I could before I got back to my friends, across the street.

Then I didn't mind sharing at all. I had already had my fill. We shared everything, even a bite of ice cream or a sip of soda. Sharing was definitely a good word to grow up with!

Hair

A comb was a supreme item for a little girl! We girls would take turns braiding each others hair. It was so great! We were little hair dressers. We were also living Barbie dolls! I always had an imitation Barbie doll, although, I once had an actual "Brand Name" doll. Her name came along with her. She was "Tressy." She had white hair that could be pulled from a hole in the top of her head. Her hair could be made longer or shorter. Girls just naturally love to comb other girl's hair. Combing a friend's hair was a real treat. But getting the tangles out was the first priority.

Painful, but once that was accomplished the reward came. Careful strokes of creating a hair style. It was so fantastic! We also shared this one comb. For some reason, we never got any itching in our hair. We didn't know about lice. They only lived in the "country" anyhow. They belonged to those country kids. Our scalps were safe for sure!

Communication from our mothers was a simple thing. A call out of a window, and we knew when it was lunch time, dinner time or just get home time!

Some of us lived on high floors. Even the kids on the lower floors would sometimes wait to take the elevator. Somehow, we felt safe with one another. We trusted each other. And we most likely didn't even know those words or their meanings. For the lower floor kids, it would have been easy enough to walk up the stairs. Their parent would be waiting outside of the corridor door right next to their apartment. This would ensure that a child would get home safely.

I lived on a lower floor. I would let my mother know of my journey as I walked up the stairs. "I'm on the second floor now!" My mother probably called back and said "Okay, hurry up!" But the elevator was a scary adventure! There were two of these imperfect boxes in each of the twelve buildings. There is nothing worst than being stuck in a non-moving elevator! Sometimes, the door would open between floors. If you were unlucky enough to be in there, you would now be staring at a concrete wall without an opening! No Way out! An alarm went off and wouldn't stop until the elevator riders were saved by either the police or the firemen! I can't remember which "uniform" men were the heroes.

While waiting to be rescued, there were no lights! Constant alarm ringing, no lights, people screaming! That's if you were fortunate enough to not be alone!

We were pretty smart children. We avoided riding the elevator all alone. This was an excellent self rule. If you are alone, total panic! Only one little voice to be unheard with the high pitch of the useless alarm. I avoided the elevator as much as possible.

It should have been called a horror chamber. Elevator? Not a good word to describe another realm! Truly not a perfect invention. Besides, there was dog urine on the elevator floor. This was constant. This was also a total mystery! Dogs were not allowed to live in the apartments. But it never failed. Dog urine!

There would be a smelly, yellow puddle and it was right smack on the middle of the elevator floor. Somewhere, a phantom dog lurked. We never saw this mysterious, invisible animal!

Staircases have to rate way above that of the horror chamber of mysterious dog urine!

Getting back to my imitation Barbie doll—She had a Barbie case, real Barbie clothes and tiny shoes that belonged to the real Barbie. Barbie didn't live in my apartment! My doll resembled the very famous Barbie. Oh, unless her limbs fell off! Then I would have a mangled doll with great clothes and— well, couldn't I have just one "real" Barbie? "Cost too much!" But with the real Barbie, you could reattach her limbs. Barbie would have lasted for years without injury! This would have been a good investment. Instead, "no brand" dolls repeatedly showed up wearing Barbie's beautiful clothes!

Dolls would sometimes journey with the small owner's "downstairs." When it rained, no problem! "Underneath" the building's entry was another entire world. It's hard to describe it. It was some type of brick overhang where different activities could go on simultaneously. Now and then, I would have to go out into the rain so my mother would know that I was okay.

The children would be on one side. Adults would be on the other side. Just hanging out and always talking about someone that wasn't there. "You know. What's her name?" "Oh, yeah. Whatchamacallit!"

Underneath the building was the entry to the

horror chamber. There were also two other doors that led to the staircases. Yet, another great place to play! On the stairs, with our combs, real Barbie's were dry and so were we! If I stayed indoors and it was raining, I had another good place to play. In my apartment we had big window-sills. I could fit myself and so many toys on the sill. I could also talk to my doll without anyone looking at me in a strange way. We had plants on the sill, also. They made great forests! Especially when I "borrowed" my brother's little toy soldiers. I would kind of borrow them, without asking (axing) either one of my brothers. It's so peculiar how playing always over-rules that of eating! A stomach could be growling for days on end. Or, so it would seem. But playing! There's nothing that can ever compare, especially when another kid would share!

Mugged!

Of course, I was too young for a "pocket-book," also known as a handbag. But I had my little two inch zippered purse which resembled a tiny little suitcase! I would use it (sometimes) when I played with any "version" of Barbie. She could almost carry it! The little suitcase housed change, I suppose. And of course, a tissue or was it a handkerchief? Either way, it was always a necessity. Kids come with runny noses. They don't have to have a cold. Moms made certain of it that their child "used something other than a sleeve!" Sleeves are so easy to use to wipe your nose. Nothing has to be pulled out of a purse. Boys had pocket. I wondered if that is where they kept their tissue or handkerchief. Sleeves were a convenience for all children. I never met one kid that didn't use their sleeve. Just show me one! It's also good in place of a napkin when you're eating. My little eyes would witness so many wondrous things!

A man would run up to an unsuspecting woman, and then within a second her handbag was now in his hand! He would also be running, real fast! The woman would be screaming! I can't remember what she was saying.

Police were very much appreciated. But children feared them! Yet, we respected them. There's nothing as good as having a policeman nearby to make a child feel safe. But firemen! In my childhood world, they ruled above police. They did everything! They had to be the tallest men known to anyone, anywhere!

My mother had great respect for them. She would tell me how brave they were. She also thought they were so...handsome!

Men did "men" things. Ladies did "lady" things. I never saw a woman as police or fire person! It just wasn't the way things were. A doctor was a man and a mother was a mom.

Girls like pink and boys like blue. Life was simpler. Life was stereotyped! But we had a "lady" crossing guard. She was dressed in a "police" uniform. I admired her! She was really good at getting us children across the street, even when the light was "red!" She led us to the sidewalk of our school.

Good old school! (Yeah, okay, sure.) The crossing guard lady was an expert at blowing her whistle to make traffic stop!

As for school, I feared it! The building was huge and dreary.

I thought that it must have been at least hundreds and hundreds of years old. It just had to be!

I had to wear a dress. Girls weren't allowed to wear slacks.

Little girls also had to (yes—had to) wear little ankle socks.

I hated them! They were, well, little. They were also pure white! They didn't seem to come in other colors. Knee high colored socks were for "bigger" girls. Ten year olds! Boy, they were so lucky!

Ready for Kindergarten! I had my brand new plaid school bag.

My big brother led me to the Kindergarten entrance. He went to his second grade entrance.

Before the children all got into the school, off I went back to my building—my safety! Legs came in very handy. Though, panic was controlling my feet. Run...!

What was I thinking? What could a five year old

be afraid of?

Simple. I wanted to be with my mother!

So for two straight days I was a Kindergarten drop out! By the third day, my mother got wise. My brother held my hand.

Oh, how embarrassing for any kid! He led me inside this time I had no choice. My legs went along with the rest of me!

I was now in…class. Hey! This isn't so bad. There were big tables and lots of chairs. And there were some toys! I don't remember seeing a blackboard. They usually were not even black.

They were green! But someone over looked that when they named them. The large room even had two bathrooms. One was boys, and the other was for girls.

We got to draw pictures. I was beginning to like this school!

Until…one day when I raised my hand to go to the bathroom.

Why is it that no matter what teachers never believe that you really need to "go?" The teacher said "No! You can go later." We all sat on our chairs in a circle. Oh, no! She should have let me go to the convenient girls room. After all, it was so close by.

My chair was the only one that had a puddle

under it! Not to mention the discomfort and embarrassment. My new dress! I wasn't sent home to change. I don't know what kind of rules the school had. But I was drenched the entire (what seemed to be days) school day. I think the teacher learned from this. The children were now asked if they had to use the bathroom. Some hands went up. Yes, it's a good idea to "ask"—or should I say "ax?"

I had to buy school cafeteria lunch. I wondered why the ladies there didn't cook as good as my mother. There was no menu. There was no choice. What was on my tray was lunch! Now the question was—"what is this stuff?"

Then on an almost empty stomach, I was expected to play outside at recess! "This is mean!" I thought. And then it was back to class for the afternoon, another few days, or so it seemed!

I always looked forward to three o'clock when the bell rang. It was finally time to go home! Yes, home...at last! I would get food that looked familiar and also had flavor to it!

My older brother and I would do homework at the kitchen table. Homework in Kindergarten? Drawing? This was great! But my brother had a notebook and pencil! Oh...my...gosh! Real homework?!

Twinkies and devil dogs with milk to snack on, too! Great food!

My younger brother was lucky. He stayed home with mom. He was too young for school. I don't think we had pre-school forty five years ago. It hadn't been "invented" yet. I only thought how lucky he was to be home! So lucky that he was three years old!

Ah! But one day he would have to venture to "school." But then I worried about him. Yes. Five year olds do worry!

I always protected him. He was, after all, my little brother!

When he was a little older, it was his turn to go to the store across the street—with dollars clutched in his hand.

He was left handed, so I suppose that's where he had the money.

One day I heard him yelling "Mom!" I ran to where he was at in the staircase and "saved" him from two boys trying to take the left handed change. I brought him home to safety. I locked the apartment door behind us. Whew! That was hard work!

I was always so alert and I always looked behind me. This was not taught to me. I just knew I had to be aware, all the time. And I was! I never got mugged. Also, if I was being followed, my fast little legs came in so handy! Believe me. At six, seven or eight years old, if I was being followed I knew it! It's just something that seems to come natural when a child is living in a large city.

I would have bad dreams and a lot of them centered on my younger brother. In these dreams, I was there for him. I was always saving him, protecting him. Especially, at Halloween time! A very bad witch was in my dream. She was trying to take him. Not with me there to help him! She never did succeed. I was like a little mother. I always thought of his safety. I don't think he remembers. That's okay. I know that at least I was there for him. I was glad for his safety, even if it was in a bad dream.

I don't recall "shoulder" strap bags. I don't even know if they were around then. Well—they should have been! To wear one properly in New York City was around the "neck" and shoulder! They were certainly not named correctly. If implied as "neck" bags, women wouldn't have their "hand bags" snatched from them!

Long straps to a pocketbook—a smart invention, and should be worn as I described. Possibly an invention that came too late for that woman that had her handbag taken by that man that ran very fast!

Summer Camp

I remember being punished by Santa Claus when he gave me that huge and staring eyed doll for Christmas!

But what did I do wrong to be sent away for two entire long weeks to summer camp? I didn't want to go! I would be on a bus with total strangers. I thought it would be okay since I would have my great books with me. My comic books of "Betty and Veronica!" They really lived a good life! They were always buying clothes and milk-shakes. What a great "book!"

I might have been anywhere between six to eight years...young. I had a little suitcase. Everything inside was brand new! I had a small case for my brand new toothbrush, toothpaste and a hair brush. Oh, and definitely a comb. A new one! I can't remember where the camp was, that's if I ever knew at all. We were surrounded by trees and frogs.

We kids had camp counselors. I wondered why they had to be mean. "Do this; do that"! "Don't do this, don't do that"! Most of all, their very famous "Don't eat with your mouth open"! I always misunderstood this. At that age, I really thought that it meant to not open your mouth at all! I would think to myself, "How can I eat anything if I can't open my mouth?" They could have given an example of what they meant. So, I would sneak the food into my little mouth. I made sure no one was looking, and then I would try to chew bit by bit. I guess I also thought they meant your lips weren't supposed to budge, either. I didn't know what they meant. It scared me! They also yelled a lot, and real loud, too!

There may have been ten girls to a cabin. And of course, one loud mouth female counselor, unlike a sweet sounding mother.

I must remark: The counselor should make sure the kids went to the bathroom before a hiking trip! I had a similar incident when I was in Kindergarten. Only this time, yuck! It came out of the other end. Very uncomfortable! It was worst than having to wear a "puddle" all day long. I could hardly walk.

I was expected to hike in this condition?!

I think I caught a glimpse of my little brother

across the way.

That was the "boys" side. I could only hope his counselor hadn't gone to "screaming" school like mine did!

Food? This doesn't resemble anything I have ever eaten before!

We shared one large bathroom. (To a little girl—everything is large!) There were no doors for the toilets. I would sneak into the bathroom in the middle of the night. Finally...privacy!

All the parents gave their children pre-stamped post cards. I don't remember what I wrote. But it had to resemble the one word—"HELP!"

Two weeks! Half of my entire life! I really don't remember what I did so wrong to deserve summer camp. At least if I was watching war movies, I was still with my family. This was much worst than those movies that my father enjoyed watching.

Betty and Veronica got me through it! But not at night when I would freeze almost to death! The itchiest blankets are only made for summer camp, and only one for each child. What are these adults thinking? Possibly freezing us to death, I bet!

I caught a big frog one day! I even put him into a shoe box. I don't know where I got the box from, but that's where he now lived. My counselor just couldn't mind her own business!

Before boarding the sacred bus home, she jabbed holes through the top lid! She said the frog needed to breathe. Well! She had to be the meanest person I ever knew! It made me also begin to realize that adults don't always know everything. They can actually be stupid! (Oh, yes they can...)

My poor frog would have done just fine without her. I cried.

One of the jabs went through him! I got him home. I buried him in a fenced in yard, right there, in front of the building. My poor frog. I knew the counselor didn't do it "on purpose." I even remember "axing" her not to put the holes in the lid.

She just wasn't very smart. I guess screaming school didn't teach her anything else, aside from yelling.

This horrible experience made me learn that I could "challenge" adults opinions and their stupid rules, too.

I had my own mind. As young as I was, I had original thought.

I had my very own...opinions!

I would never let my parents, ever again, send me to that camp.

I voiced my discord. I voiced what "I" thought.

Sometimes, my voicing got me into trouble. "Don't talk back to adults!"

My response: "Everyone is not nice. Everyone is not...smart."

I can't remember if my little brother brought a "murdered" frog home. Maybe one day I'll "ax" him.

Oh, yes! My wonderful home with my family! No stupid people live here. Especially, no simple minded, yelling camp counselors! Back to my toys, real food, and a warm blanket.

I was now eating recognizable food, again. A bologna sandwich!

Now, that's food! I didn't waste one bite of it, either. I might have eaten the crust, too! Bread crust to kids was a no-no, but I was starving!

I asked my mother "How can a person eat when they can't open their mouth?" I explained to my mother what the counselor said.

My mother was pretty smart. In a few moments she did explain it. But I needed more information. I needed someone to perform this impossible maneuver. So my older brother showed me what the counselor meant. Sure, now I got it! That was easy enough.

It was so strange that an adult couldn't explain it that simple!

Now I was back with my "gang." My good friends! I could hardly wait to get my hair done by one of them! This time, though, I could let them use my "new" comb. Well, it was still "kind of new."

I even appreciated my fake Barbie doll. She was still waiting there in the real Barbie's case. And just as mangled as when I left her before I went away to a child's "nightmare!"

Picnics!

Summer picnics were the best! My family and my little self went to Staten Island. The other boroughs of New York City were considered "the country." Only truly Manhattan was the "City!" We attended "Greek" picnics on Staten Island. We went there by way of Ferry. What an adventure! A huge boat on the East River! It seemed like an endless ocean. This was great! The river's wind was the best part of the trip! At the end of the ferry's trip, we all got picked up by car driven by a relative. A Greek relative! Then we were taken somewhere (on this Island) to have a big picnic with relatives. I don't remember if it would be any special occasion. But that was where the Greek picnics were, anyhow.

There was music in a very unusual language. I never understood any of the words. I didn't speak much Greek. The music had a kind of good beat, though! The same dance was done over and over, again. Everyone held hands and danced in a crooked circle. It was fun! Lamb! I never did eat it. I got sick to my stomach by the smell. I was possibly the only Greek which never liked lamb. Anyone that knew me could confirm this as a fact!

At these picnics I only ate the desserts. What delicious ones at that! Every single bite had honey in it. A child's dream! The pastry was the best part of these picnics. Also seeing my family that lived there was good, too. I don't remember much more. I had to have been really young. I probably didn't even have a half of a year added to my age. That's how young I was!

Baptist Church picnics were the greatest!

My neighbors always invited me with them to these. I guess they invited me because I was such "a good little girl." I wondered about the "good" part!

The Baptist Church sponsored them. There were so many buses.

And the food had to be, by far, the best food on the planet!

There was so much of it, too! All of the mothers made the food themselves. They were really good cooks! For me to eat their cooking—they must have been the best cooks!

God lived everywhere. That's what I was taught.

When you're a child, religion didn't interfere with friendship. Adults sure could learn a lot from children!

I always looked forward to these picnics. Baseball, kick ball, all of this with the nicest strangers. People that didn't even know me were feeding me! All of the kids played together. Even with the boys! Yes! How else can a little girl play a boy sport if she weren't playing with boys? They didn't seem to mind, either. I was really good at games played with a ball.

Even football! Baseballs hurt the most, though. I know for sure that these hard balls gave painful "black eyes!" But the game was fun. I enjoyed boy's games almost as much as combing my friend's hair. Even almost as much as using nail polish for paint! Sports were definitely a fantastic invention!

The potato salad was great. Globs of mayonnaise and eggs! I could have lived on potato salad the rest of my life!

The food alone was worth coming along for! My neighbor's mom always made sure I got fed. Her potato salad rated number one!

I don't know where we all were. But I know that the kindest and happiest people were there with me!

Music, dancing! Even singing! All of this was

going on at the same time. Never a dull moment!

These were the greatest picnics on the planet, yet I don't have one single photograph to show for it. I'm sure in someone's memory book (in The Smith) there are photo's of...me! Maybe some little children are looking at them and wondering... "Hey, mommy. Who is that little girl with the black eye?"

I do have my childhood memories. I remember a lot of the good things. I do also remember the bad. As a child, the good things were a lot better than the bad things. Bad things were a lot worst than any war movie that I ever watched!

Oh, yes! The best grape Kool-Aid drink known to humankind was also at these picnics! Yummm! So much sugar! I knew what I would be dreaming about that night! Food and grape drink.

It's strange. I ate a lot as a child. Yet, my mother specially bought for me some yucky liquid chalk stuff called "Weight On."

Maybe my mother wasn't making that great potato salad. She was probably making too much...lamb! (Yuck!)

Scars

There was one popular question every girl asked their mother. Perhaps, the number one question asked everywhere. I'm not sure if boys asked their fathers this question. "Where do babies come from?"

The second most important question for a "project" kid was "Can I have a bike, please?" Well, my mother answered the second question quickly enough! "No. You can't have a bike. We have no room for bikes." That was easy. I wanted a "boys" ten speed bike! I would borrow one, now and then. I would also always fall off! I have great scars to prove it, too! Scars were important to children; maybe it was some sort of hurting victory. Like when a kid wins a fight or something. I just don't know the reason. But scars were real important when I was growing up. It was even more important if the scars belonged to a...girl! Not too many girls had scars like I had! That's because I was more daring then they were. I actually rode boy's bikes. I was braver than other little girls.

Across the street and around the corner was a bike rental shop. I could never figure out why it was called a "Fix it shop." I just rented a bike there. I would soon find out why the rental shop had "fix" in its name.

The chains always fell off right in the middle of riding them! No doubt about it! These were the worst bikes ever made!

Some of my neighbor's had bikes. In fact, that would be the very first thing your legs ran into when you entered their apartment! Though, they do a lot of damage to the legs, they leave great scars! Now that I think about it, scars were important for me to have because they proved that wasn't a "sissy!" The more scars, the less you got picked on. Especially, when a boy would almost like you. Then he would see the scars and be jealous. Yes! Jealous. Scars played a very big role in a child's life. They were worn with pride! The deeper the better and I sure had good ones, too!

Now, getting back to that "first" well asked question. "Where do babies come from?" The answer would be "When you have your own, you'll know." Good answer, I suppose. The "stork" was never brought into the conversation, even though the conversation consisted of one question, and one sentence as an answer.

I saw on cartoons, when the channel wasn't wiggling, a stork delivering a baby to its parents. I wondered what type of bird could be allowed to fly babies away from... Heaven? I put babies out of my mind. Where they came from wasn't as important as great, painful, oozing with pus and blood scars! Buildings in New York City are either built with bricks or concrete, or both. There is always the painful corner wall trims made of steel.

In The Smith, twelve, seventeen story brick buildings towered with perfection. I don't know if sheet rock was invented, yet. If it had been, it wasn't used in any New York City buildings!

Only the hardest metals were used. Concrete walls! I would watch as my father tackled with a wall all day, just to get one nail hammered in.

Well, it just couldn't be done! So he brought out machinery for this job. A drill; fascinating tool! Anchors came in handy, too. But they could never be removed. Amazing!

We would all be assured that mirror wasn't going to fall off the wall. Not ever. My father made sure of that!

I did wonder why there were so many chips taken out of the paint?

Either way, that mirror had to be put up. Something had to cover up all of those other marks that were now on that wall.

My most valiant scar came from a children's game called "monster."

My neighbor's brother was the monster. We were little girls.

Girls were not monsters! He ran after us, down his hallway, in their apartment. I turned around to see how close he was to catching me, then I looked back the other way and...bammmm!

I ran into the corner of a wall, the corner that had the steel!

I remember seeing a lot of blood, and then I passed out.

I opened my eyes slightly and saw a bright light. No! Not the after-life. I knew I was in a hospital.

I had a crack in my forehead! I passed out, again. I don't know how or when I got home. My parents must have been worried out of their minds!

I had stitches in my forehead. I didn't count them. But the accident left a most unique scar!

Well, I can say for sure, I never played monster

again. I also never ran in an apartment after that! I'm not that stupid!

For certain, those projects were built very strong, and very much built with pride. The Smith will always be a part of me. After all, its mark is forever on my forehead!

The Zoo

Downtown Manhattan had so many exciting fun things to offer!

Central Park was nice. My family and I would have outings there. We would take a train. If you were small enough to fit underneath the turnstiles, you didn't need a token. Small kids could ride the train for free!

It's scary being beneath the ground. I did enjoy the breeze that came as the train was approaching.

I think we had to walk far to the Zoo, once we got into Central Park. Then again, I had little legs. Maybe, it wasn't so far.

I loved seeing the amazing animals. I don't know which was my favorite. They probably all were! I didn't like their homes, though. Cages! Small cages. They didn't have much room to walk around. They couldn't run. I knew I would not be happy if I ever had to live in a cage.

I wondered why these animals couldn't be brought to that great place in New Jersey. Maybe the Zoo people didn't know about it.

Maybe they should have learned about it! The animals really didn't look happy in those cages.

It didn't really make me feel happy, either. Were cages really a good invention? I could only wish for them to one day find New Jersey! I don't think it was too far away.

Central Park had a nice lake with ducks. They weren't caged.

I wanted so much to swim in the lake. It wasn't allowed.

Then why was it...there?

Back in the train heading home, I would fall asleep to the rocking motion and roaring of the train.

"Wake up! We're there!"

Then from the train, more walking. Oh! There's my building.

Oh, no. Not that! We're going to take—the elevator! We waited long enough for it, we could have been home hours ago.

Or, so it seemed. But I was probably right. Hours...!

It wasn't too bad waiting. We would get to see a lot

of our neighbors. Everyone was complaining about the elevator being so slow to come down from the higher floors. Mostly, adults talked in length about that elevator. I could have easily said "Then take the stairs!" But I was much better mannered than that.

Okay, here we go—inside a cramped chamber! And they really called this thing that we were in "a ride." "An elevator ride!"

Whoever added the word ride to elevator probably never went to Coney Island. Those were real "rides!"

On with the bathing suits, in with the bubble bath, and of course our battleships! Afterwards, a nice home cooked meal.

My mother always said "It's a great life!" I didn't realize what she meant. I guess she was grateful for the little things.

There was always food on our table. My father worked hard.

My mother took good care of us and the apartment.

Throughout my three to eight year old mind, I can remember lots of friends. Ice cream trucks! Fresh ice cream! Not frozen stuff that came in a box, either.

I wonder if anyone in my family knew that I could be found under the kitchen table when I didn't want dinner. Hmmm...

Then there was the knish man pushing his hot oven on wheels down a street. Sometimes, for us children, he actually came up on the sidewalk! I guess that he didn't want us getting hurt by a car. The best knishes around came from one nice man. For a nickel he sold half a knish. He'd place it, steaming hot, in a paper bag. He drowned it with lots of salt. Lots of it! Fantastic meal right there in a little brown bag. I had a whole half of a knish just for me! A knish is kind of hard to describe. The outside has sort of

a breading. They are square and have mashed potatoes inside of them!

We weren't rich. We weren't poor. I only knew that if we needed something, we would have it. My parent's always seen to that. I might have watched a lot of those war movies, but I also remember the hugs. Hugs are one of the finest inventions!

Lit Up!

I was very young, so of course I could not venture out at night. But to be with my parents at night, my little eyes saw the best of all sights!

The City would be lit up with many lights! There were car lights. Street lights, even late night store lights. The best ever was the Brooklyn Bridge lights! My thoughts to this could only be "How pretty!" There was no fear there. Not to my recollection. Safety was being with my parents, and oh, so many bright lights! They resembled stars that were very close by.

Lights surrounded The Smith from all around. It was like the buildings were within a circle of lit up protection. Beautiful shining protection!

In Brooklyn, the place of the greatest lights was at Coney Island! Every single ride was all lit up! Great night wonderment! Everyone went to Coney Island. I'm pretty sure it was mostly in the summer.

Summer was great in the "city of lights." Although, as I said before—only Manhattan was The City!

The other boroughs were so different. Their buildings didn't tower. But Brooklyn had a kids world all its own. Which ride do we go on first? Oh, there were so many to choose from! My favorite was the carousel, or the "Merry-Go-Round!" Beautiful, stiff horses painted so many colors. I always got on the big horse that was on the outside. I was brave! If a person reached there arm out far enough, they could try to grab a brass ring.

I was tiny. I couldn't reach the ring. But I did so try!

There were belts that held kids and adults onto the horses.

Carousel horse belts were a good invention!

Once in a while, only an adult would reach and grab the brass ring. I didn't know if they got a prize. I only saw that it was great to get this circle that shined.

To me it was a golden ring. I think people would clap their hands when someone actually reached out and got it!

They had to have the longest arms. It was impossible for a child to ever even come close to reaching it.

I was not disappointed if I could never grab it. I stayed so proud on my big, beautiful horse. I held up my head and I was riding with this horse as we felt the warm wind!

And the music! It was the loudest that I ever heard! When it began to quiet down, I knew my horse and I would be stopping soon.

My parents bought me and my brothers yet another ticket to ride.

I chose another horse this time. An inside horse. I didn't need the outside horse. I would never be able to grab the gold ring.

The inside horses were great, too! I got "belted" in by some man and away we rode! I would look back to try to see my brothers and their horses. I thought my horse was better than theirs!

My horse had both front legs up. How daring I was!

There were some large seats in the middle of the carousel. They must have been for people that didn't like to ride horses. Or, for people that were just tired. Best of all, the ride shined with lights! What an amazing night adventure! (Just to think that some people called the elevator a "ride!")

As for the Ferris wheel, I just wasn't allowed on it

at all. A man would measure a kid's height. I was too small. That was okay with me!

I simply enjoyed watching this circle of seats which went all the way up to the sky! If I watched the lights spin around, I found my head was spinning, too!

The Ferris wheel had to be the biggest ride I had ever seen!

The seats also rocked. Yes! I was glad I was too small to make that trip. Very, very glad! I did enjoy what was called the Kiddy Rides.

Little boats attached to one another, going around in a circle.

Boy, there were a lot of circle things at Coney Island!

The boats were on water. I remember stepping into one. I panicked! There was a giant size bug in my boat! My legs seemed to leave my body. One leg went into the water! I don't know who saved me. But I never went on the boat ride ever again. I'll just stick to dry land Kiddy Rides!

The "Cyclone," also called The Roller Coaster, had to be the noisiest ride of them all! It was mostly of noise of people that were screaming! They really should have named it "The Screaming Ride!" And if they were so scared why did they go on again?

I could only hope that my parents didn't buy me a ticket for that one! Oh, great! They didn't. Of course the measuring man, once again, turned me away. How about that?! A child that was actually "happy" not to be able to go on the Roller Coaster!

I thought that it was a good thing to be too small. I was very glad that I could only go on the Kiddy Rides. Oh, except the boat ride with the big bugs!

After all that excitement, my brothers and I would sleep for a long time! Of course, that was when we finally got home.

We had to take a train all the way out of Brooklyn to Manhattan.

It took hours and hours and even more hours! Or, so it seemed to me. Then of course—yes! We would take a bus at night from the train. Oh, great! My feet just couldn't walk anymore.

Sometimes we got into a yellow car. The car had letters on the doors that read—"TAXI"

We got to The Smith very fast in that yellow car! My parents called it "a cab." I don't think that is what it was. I know that it began with the "T" letter, not "C" letter.

I remember being carried the rest of the way. I was probably falling asleep.

I only remember waking up the next morning to

the wonderful smell of bacon and pancakes with syrup. What a wonderful smell!

Adults seemed to like the smell, also. I liked my breakfast with milk.

My mother was always so prepared. How did she know that we would be so hungry? Home made pancakes and sweet, thick syrup! The syrup was really good when you dipped your bacon in it. Sloppy, but very sweet bacon. Yummy!

Nothing came out of a box. Nothing came out of the freezer.

All home made food made by my mother's own hands!

One thing did come out of a can, especially in winter. It was very popular in every child's home. Campbell's soup!

It wasn't complete without little oyster crackers. Good meal, but not my mother's home made beef stew!

My Mom would try to trick me when it was lamb stew. I knew the smell was different. Don't adults know that a kid's nose cannot be tricked? My mom would take out the carrots and potatoes and rinse them off with water. I ate those. Just as long as no lamb was sneaked into my bowl.

Coney Island was a true child's wonderland!

It was great in the day time. That would be not at the beach or ocean and no "sand" sandwiches for us! The boardwalk held the most delicious food.

Nathan's hot dogs and freshly cut potatoes fried in a deep pot of grease.

The best, biggest French fries were at Coney Island. No one could resist these. And they had an endless supply of them! The fries just kept coming. People and kids just kept eating! Coney Island had to be the supreme invention of a child's life! I could only wonder why Manhattan couldn't have rides, too. I think a Carousel was at the Zoo. But one ride isn't as great as millions of rides. Big rides that went up to the sky!

The prettiest yellow flowers grew on the grass every summer in The Smith. They were fun to pick. They never lasted long when I put them in a glass of water. I now know that they were weeds! I was between the ages of five to eight, but these were free flowers! I didn't have to pay any cents for them! I thought that they were pretty, too! Such a nice, bright yellow color! If a kid was six or seven, a very important half of a year was so very important. For example: "I'm not six! I'm six and a half!"

There was also the younger version of "I'm six and one fourth!" Fractions learned by that much needed extra one fourth, or a half, made mathematics much easier to learn at school. My brothers and I did well at school. Though, smartness went in an order of age, or so it seemed. My older brother was the smartest. I was the second smartest. My little brother, smart, but left handed!

I'm not including my sister in this "smartest list" because she was "older."

It was thought that to be left handed, a child couldn't be so smart. Of course, this was not true. Hey! We were kids; we understood what we were told.

It was fun playing left handed, though. I wrote pretty well when I taught my left hand to go along with my "penmanship." Yes! That's what writing was known by. It was kind of a scary word! But that's just what it was in school books.

There was always a night light in our apartment hallway and kitchen. Whether adult or child, everyone got up at night either to go to the bathroom, or to get a drink of milk. If I got lucky, there would be chocolate milk in our fridge! Sweet, brown, thick liquid chocolate in a milk container! Night lights are a good idea. Chocolate milk, much better! We were smart kids. We knew that there were no cows that gave chocolate milk. In fact, we didn't know cows gave milk. I only knew milk, like juice, came in a container from "The Store." Most likely, a store from across the street! We also had a milk man deliver milk, and a seltzer man who delivered seltzer and sweet syrup to make your own milk shakes!

Flash lights were great, too! But they only worked with batteries. Under the covers, comic book and a flashlight!

We must have had a lot of flash lights. My brothers enjoyed this same ritual, too! After we were tucked in, at least one of my parents made their rounds. (Shhh! Flashlights off!)

We all had our own flashlights. That was a good idea. My parents thought ahead. They must have known that three children, two boys and a girl, were not about to share one single flashlight. They were so very right!

There must have been a hidden, parent alarm bell that let them know we were reading after being tucked in. A mystery! I never found this hidden "tattle-tail!" It must have been hidden up high, where a small child couldn't see it—all the way up there!

Well, we were kids. The flash lights were turned on just for a little bit longer. We had to finish our books. That's "comic" books!

Chicken Pox

I don't know how me and my brothers did it, but we all had the chicken pox at the same time!

I remember feeling fine. I only had a little bit of an itch and a few dots on my face. They really should have been called the itchy pox or anything other "chicken." Chickens had nothing to do with these bumps!

It was great being put into my parent's bed with my brothers in the day time. I guess my mother had to keep an eye on all of us at the same time. So, their bed was big enough for the three of us "sick kids!" We actually got along, too. Being sick seems to do that to children. Or maybe we were just happy that we didn't have to go to school! That was most likely the true reason that we were getting along without "fighting!" We would watch the "up and down" T.V. that my father watched his movies on. We didn't get any sleep. When you're sick, that's what you're supposed to do. But nope, not us! T.V. all day and toast with jelly. I guess it was the only food that a kid could eat when they got sick. The jelly was good. It was kind of like thick, clumpy syrup. But it always slid off of the toast. Messy!

"Don't scratch! You'll have scars." Pink calamine lotion to the rescue! For days, the three of us were covered with coatings of pink wet stuff. When it dried, I think that it made the itch worst! Why did it have to be pink? And as for scars, what could be so bad about that?!

I'm sure, at the time, if my mother got sick she never said anything. I can now only imagine how many headaches she must have gotten! Hey, we're children. We think a lot about ourselves!

I would help my mom clean, dust and do dishes. I had to stand on a chair to reach the sink. I liked doing dishes. Bubbles were for the kitchen sink, too! Not only for bath time. I had made my very own..."discovery!"

Sweet smelling soap was used on the dishes. I don't remember anything coming out of a soap container. I think Ivory soap was the dish cleaner. Whatever soap it was, it was fun! When I was done, I got to play with toys in the kitchen sink. I also played with that soap. It actually "floated!" Oh, yes it did! It became an instant soap boat for little passengers. I can't recall what toys I played with, but my brothers were placed on chairs and joined in with the Ivory soap, kitchen sink fun! My mother stood by with the kitchen mop. We probably flooded the kitchen floor. It was great!

Water was definitely on my list of great things! And bubbles were a big plus—mixed in with toys!

Fun got even better if our friends "next door" were sick, too! Outside the apartments was a very long hallway.

One basketball and lots of sick kids in a hallway playing! What a great place to live in! Of course, we had those mean neighbors that told on us. The Housing Policeman would come up and tell us to stop with the noise. He was nice, so we listened to him. The mystery was "Who told on us?! They had to be the meanest neighbor!

My favorite holiday was Halloween! Though, I'm not sure I did pronounce it correctly. Let's see: How-low-ween. That sounds pretty close.

Trick or treating was easy and safe. We kids never even had to leave the building! A bunch of us stayed on "our floor" going door to door. Parents all stood with open doors with a big bowl of all kinds of candy! We were allowed to take what we wanted, too!

Costumes were usually hand made by mothers. I thought it would be nice to have a mask bought from a store.

I was either a princess or something pretty. Boys were the ones with scary masks! Boys were definitely scarier than girls could ever be! That's the way it was. Girls wore pretty costumes.

Boys were monsters! This rule was easily accepted. Especially, by the boys. They just have "this thing" about scaring girls.

Carving pumpkins was an art my father performed. He was a true artist! He used a "curved" knife. My father made the best creations from a big, orange thing!

But Easter egg time, my older brother was the greatest "egg dyer." No one could surpass his egg art! He made "rainbow" colored eggs! I could never figure out how he never got the dye all blended together. He made separate rows of colors.

I can only guess that's where the saying "Like father like son" comes into play. It's an adult saying!

The fun part was having "egg" fights. Real easy game!

Each of us had a hard boiled, rainbow colored egg. Hand held, who could "crack" the other's first?! I won only half of the time.

But it was fun eating the eggs! After the shell was massacred, we ate distorted colored eggs. The dye went through the shell.

They still tasted like eggs. I especially liked egg salad. Mayonnaise and colored eggs smashed together on bread! The crust was never eaten for some unknown reason. Bread end crust just wasn't for children to eat. What an inconvenience this was. Bread should have been made without the crust! My mother always had the job of cutting off the crust. She would feed it to the birds (pigeons) that were on the outside window sill. They sure ate a lot. They ate anything that they were given! I should know because my mother was a great crust cutter. Mom used a knife! That's why it was her job. Children weren't supposed to use knives. It's so odd that a child can still find the strength to play when they are "sick." Faking sick wasn't such a bad idea, either! That's when a kid didn't want to go to school. Then, a child could play all day! "You're going to school tomorrow!" Oh, no! I'd quickly stop playing and got into bed! Maybe I can pretend to be sick "better" next time! First grade was a true punishment for me. My teacher was the "real" wicked witch from the west. Oh, yes she was! She looked just like that witch from the "Wizard of Oz" movie. She was very mean to me. She didn't like me. I didn't like her, either. I probably "hated" her! But this word was not familiar to a six and a half year old.

I remember my mother meeting with school adults. That teacher and me were there, too.

That wicked teacher said that I never raised my hand in class. She also said that I never spoke out. She said, and I do remember so clearly, that I must be "retarded." That was a fact!

The "fact" was what the teacher had actually said about me; not that I was really retarded.

My mother's few words proved this teacher very wrong.

My mom said "Samantha doesn't raise her hand much because she is shy. But most importantly, she doesn't "speak out" in class because I raised her to be a polite, little lady!"

Mother's can be great rescuers! And my mother was right. I was lucky that she defended me. Also, that it was the end of the first grade. I would be going to a smart second grade class.

I might have been tested for intelligence, I don't remember. I only know that if my mother hadn't been at that meeting, my life would have been ruined by a wicked, mean witch!

When one of us was sick, my mom wrote the nicest "excuse from school" notes! She would begin by writing: Dear Mrs. (Whatever the teacher's name was.) Then followed by: "Kindly excuse..."

The meeting episode might have sparked my thoughts that adults could be wrong, too! That might have been when I learned to "speak up; defend myself. To...question adults.

If this wicked teacher was so wrong about me, how many other adults were not perfect? I would be careful. I would raise my hand from then on, but only if I knew the answer!

Sometimes, teachers would tell me to give another student a chance to answer. My answers must have been correct!

Original thought was certainly meant to question an adult. I know now that they didn't always have the right answers.

After all, the teachers had answers in their books! This was not for us students. If the teachers needed answers in their books, they may not have "known" the answer!

My education was now going on the right path— To question adults. What a concept! What a learning experience for a child. Wisdom doesn't only come with age! Wisdom comes from experience;

knowing what is right and knowing that "they" are possibly wrong.

I knew I had to let my future teachers know that I had the answers. I studied. I excelled! Though, I didn't have the words "to excel" in my vocabulary. I knew I had to "show them" that I was smart, and I succeeded!

Getting back to being "sick" is a hard thing when parents don't believe you!

Okay. We had no medical staff at elementary school. The Principal made the phone calls home to parents.

"Yes, Mrs. so and so—Your daughter threw up! She might have a fever, too." What was this man? Some sort of nurse in disguise? Many times children don't lie. The ones that do must hear constant lies at home!

If I say I'm sick, believe me. Oh, and to comment on "baby" aspirin: It might have been "chewable", but it tasted like chalk! Somewhere in my life time, I must have eaten chalk before. I seem to compare it to quite a bit of other "edible" items! I was afraid for my younger brother when he started Kindergarten! Kids pronounced it as "Kindergarden." There was no such garden anywhere to be found! There was just a large room with a lot of kids. The

Kindergarten teachers were kind of nice. I could only hope that my brother would be brave. I believe that he was.

The Question

I don't know why and perhaps others don't know either—There is an age old question that is asked of every child.

"What do you want to be when you grow up?"

Well, more than forty years ago, a boy wanted to be a doctor.

A boy didn't want to grow up to get married nor have children.

Girls, on the other hand, wanted to get married and have children.

Or, maybe that's what they were told that they had to do.

Eight year olds have a good imagination. As an eight year old I thought girls had to become mothers! And that they were never doctors. That was simply how it was. Could anyone really have imagined me saying "I want to be...President?!"

Only boys could wish for that.

I did know I wanted to help people. Maybe kids gave the answer that they knew adults wanted to hear. That makes some kind of sense in an eight year old mind. Maybe I would have a better conception, of the answer to this often asked question, when I'm eight and a half. Better yet, when I'm eight and three fourths years old!

One thing I did know was that I would speak up if I was being told the wrong thing! I could control my voice. I could say "no." Or even, "that's not nice."

Adults don't seem to appreciate it when a child has an "opinion."

I never spoke back to adults. My parents taught me not to. Ah!

But that's when I was "little!"

Just like the word "mankind", itself. Doesn't anyone else know there are girls and ladies, too? "Humankind" in my time was never heard.

Yet, it was a truth. Boys and girls, including adults, were all human. So, why label "kind" as "mankind?"

I don't think I even considered this one opinion to adults, no less, teachers. I probably would have gotten some horrible punishment! A typical school punishment was being sent to the Principal's office. As long as he didn't have a T.V., that was fine. Also if I was called "white," even at that early age, I rebelled! "I'm not white. I'm...beige. See my skin next to this milk? Milk is "white!"

Colors! Either way, at least try and get it right!

Adults had it so wrong. Only a few people that I saw had their skin white. They also got sunburn real bad, too! I would become a beautiful light milk chocolate color in the summer. That's when adults would ask my mother, right in front of me, if I was adopted?! How awful to put such a thought into a small child's head! So then I wondered if I was I adopted! It is said that children can be so cruel. I know, for a fact, that adults can be much crueler! And some adults say "bad" words a lot of the time!

A little guidance from the right adult can be so helpful. Those several innocent years were perhaps some of my best years! I had learned so much. Not only from school work, but I learned a lot about life itself. Adults were not perfect, for one! What do I want to be when I grow up? My answer: Smart!

If I believed something was wrong, I would question.

My punishment at home for questioning—being put in a corner of my parents room while my father watched "war movies."

I'm a little girl. John Wayne was almost always in

these "punishment movies!"

"Oh, no! Not my little brother, too! What did he do?"

"I have a plan. When my dad goes to the kitchen— I'll call for help!" My plan always worked!

My mother would come to our rescue! We would be released from the "war movie chamber!"

I'm sure my parents meant me no harm. I suppose any concept of a child telling an "adult" that they are wrong—just wasn't a good thing in the very early 1960's.

I do remember that they were proud of me, though. They did show me off to people! I was so cute!

White ankle socks made a school outfit complete. I didn't like them. Little girls couldn't wear "knee high" socks until they were older. There was always that one girl who couldn't resist kicking those ankle socks. I would go home with dirty ankle socks.

I voiced! I raised my hand to the teacher! I told on the girl.

That was a most proud achievement for a child! She never got my socks dirty after that!

I believed if I didn't have the "guts" to tell, my parents would "embarrass" me and show up at school! Good motivation for a child: Avoiding embarrassment. So speak up for yourself, kids!

Curls

I had chestnut brown, long straight hair. Why on earth would my mother want my hair to be curly?! There was only one way to get it curly. My mother lit the stove. She placed within the fire a terrible invention! A hot "curling" iron! I could smell my hair burning. It stunk! I could hear my hair making a crackling noises! "Mom. That was my ear, not my hair." "Oh, I'll be more careful." Horror from an instrument of some type of metal, my bangs got the torture, too! So did part of my forehead! I had bangs to cover up that great scar from the playing "monster" game at the neighbor's apartment incident.

The worst thing about hot hair curls is that you can't comb your hair afterwards. Oh, no you can't! I was glad when they were gone. Shampoo and water. As I said earlier, water is great! But bubbles in the hair are better!

Hair could be shaped in all sorts of ways as long as it was wet, with shampoo lathered all over it. It was a lot of fun making pointy hair-dos by myself!

I wasn't Shirley Temple. I didn't want to be. But I was a good dancer! There was no special name to the dancing that I did. I just danced. I made up my own moves. I could sing a little. But I'd rather dance. Dancing was even better with a ponytail. It flopped about as my head moved! Ponytails were great. Braids were even better! Pig tails weren't so great. Hair ribbons were good. Plastic hair "things" that held the hair back were painful! They were hard and had "teeth" that held (bit) onto the hair! The teeth dug into the scalp. Why would anyone ever invent such a painful thing for hair?! There were many colors to choose from. But by the end of a school day I had dizziness with a headache!

It was like magic when the hard head band was removed! The dizziness and headache were instantly gone! Hard head bands with teeth were not a very pleasant invention. A pony tail joined with a braid was a supreme hair-do. And it was not painful! My sister taught me how to braid my own hair. This was better than tying shoes! Rubber bands and ribbons were a girl's necessity! As for curls—I didn't want them!

In my later years, I advanced to hair barrettes and bobby-pins. Although, there's nothing like a good, strong rubber band! I used the kind that I also used to make that great Chinese jump rope. How versatile rubber bands were! Then there was the material, somewhat stretchable, hair band. It was less painful than the hard ones with teeth that dug into my skull! But again—too tight, instant pain would arrive!

No hair accessory can ever compare to a rubber band. They did snap, sometimes. That's when my fingers got the snapping pain.

Another rubber band and presto!

I suppose they could fall under the category of "magic!"

At least they didn't claw their way straight into my brain!

Books

My favorite books were of Greek Mythology. I even had a Greek alphabet book. I taught myself how to carefully come up with words using these similar letters to the "regular" alphabet. The Greek Gods were great! My favorite Goddesses were Athena, Goddess of War. Aphrodite, Goddess of Love and Beauty. And Terpsichore, Goddess of Song and Dance! She was one of the nine muses of "inspiration."

I'm not sure if I realized then that the Romans renamed the Greek Gods. But I did know Aphrodite was not "Venus!" And Hercules was the Roman name for Heracles. One day, maybe someone will get it right!

Comic books were the best! Some of the words I was able to read. But the colorful pictures alone were quite enough for a child! Comic books were the best books! They could even be read under the covers, brought on vacation and shared with friends! They could even be…traded! Or, a kid could even borrow a comic from a friend.

Adults don't think too highly of them. But if you want to get a child to read—definitely give them comic books! They contain so many adventures!

Even a child's dreams had the characters in them. Comic books rate very high on my scale of great things! I suppose they could be considered "inventions." "Great things" were a better description and more deserving for comic books.

They could even be folded and put into a pocket! But that's only if you had pockets!

A great child's pass time, especially when sick, (yes, you guessed right) were comic books! My father bought me and my brothers the comic books we liked when we were sick.

Wow, a "reward" for being sick! What could be greater? Getting better, if you were really sick. Then I could truly enjoy these great comic stories! I found it amazing that comic books had colored pictures. So why couldn't the same color be added to our black and white (really more of a grey) T.V? Of course, my brothers had their "Superman" comic books. These I would venture into only when Lois Lane was on the front cover. Hey, I'm a girl! I liked seeing what she was wearing! I also didn't think that she went through the torture of using a hot curling iron on her hair! The very last age of my childhood story is eight years old. With all of the adventures and great inventions, what more could an eight year old girl want? Easy answer: "To be nine years old!"

The Lower East Side of Manhattan is now part of "Tribeca," (whatever that might mean!) Personally, I think that the "Down-Town" Manhattan area should keep the name it always had. There's a very old saying... "Leave good enough alone!" That saying should apply here.

Perhaps, Tribeca sounds better to the "elite!" This way, they can separate themselves from the true "natives" that live there. The natives are known as the working class people!

I still visit The Smith now and then. The stores "across the street" are now mostly restaurants. Everything is no longer sold there. I believe that the restaurants are for visitors. The beautiful Church is still there. Though, the Priest locks the doors now, after mass.

The East River will always be there, I hope. With enough imagination, one can still envision The Beast from 20,000 Fathoms coming out of the river and eating people!

Old buildings are now "luxury" apartments. The South Street Seaport was built when I was still growing up. It used to be just a smelly fish market!

Some of my friends are still around. Some of my family is still there, too!

Chinatown is now separated by "Little Italy." To me...it is one in the same!

The Two Towers are gone. So are some good people that I grew up with. I have a framed poster of The Two Towers of when they were first built. I believe a pizzeria had been there first.

The Brooklyn Bridge is in the poster, also. The other side of the Bridge is where I lived; where I grew up. I will always be so very proud of where I was raised. I wouldn't want to have grown up anywhere else! Manhattan made me the person that I am today. Without New York City, I don't even hesitate to wonder who I would be.

I remember my childhood tears, my scrapes and my scars. I will always remember the hugs!

My parents and my Aunt have been gone now for a long time. They are resting forever...in New Jersey.

When I was seventeen, I met a great guy in The Smith! He lived in one of those "bad" buildings. He wasn't anywhere near "bad." He was...sweet! I am so glad that I thought about it and gave him a "second look." Two years later, I married him! We talk about his childhood, too. We raised our children with our childhood stories. It fascinated them!

Several years ago...my sons and husband gave me a very special gift. It was my very first (and last) "Barbie" doll!

We live far away, now. Though, New York City will always be a part of us...most sincerely.

Irreplaceable

We meet new friends,
though we may part.
Best of friends stay
within your heart.

Endearing family is...
irreplaceable!
Sweet memories can never
be taken from you...

CPSIA information can be obtained at www.ICGtesting.com
Printed in the USA
BVOW02s1414060514

352729BV00001B/44/P